THE ART OF SANDRA CHANG-ADAIR

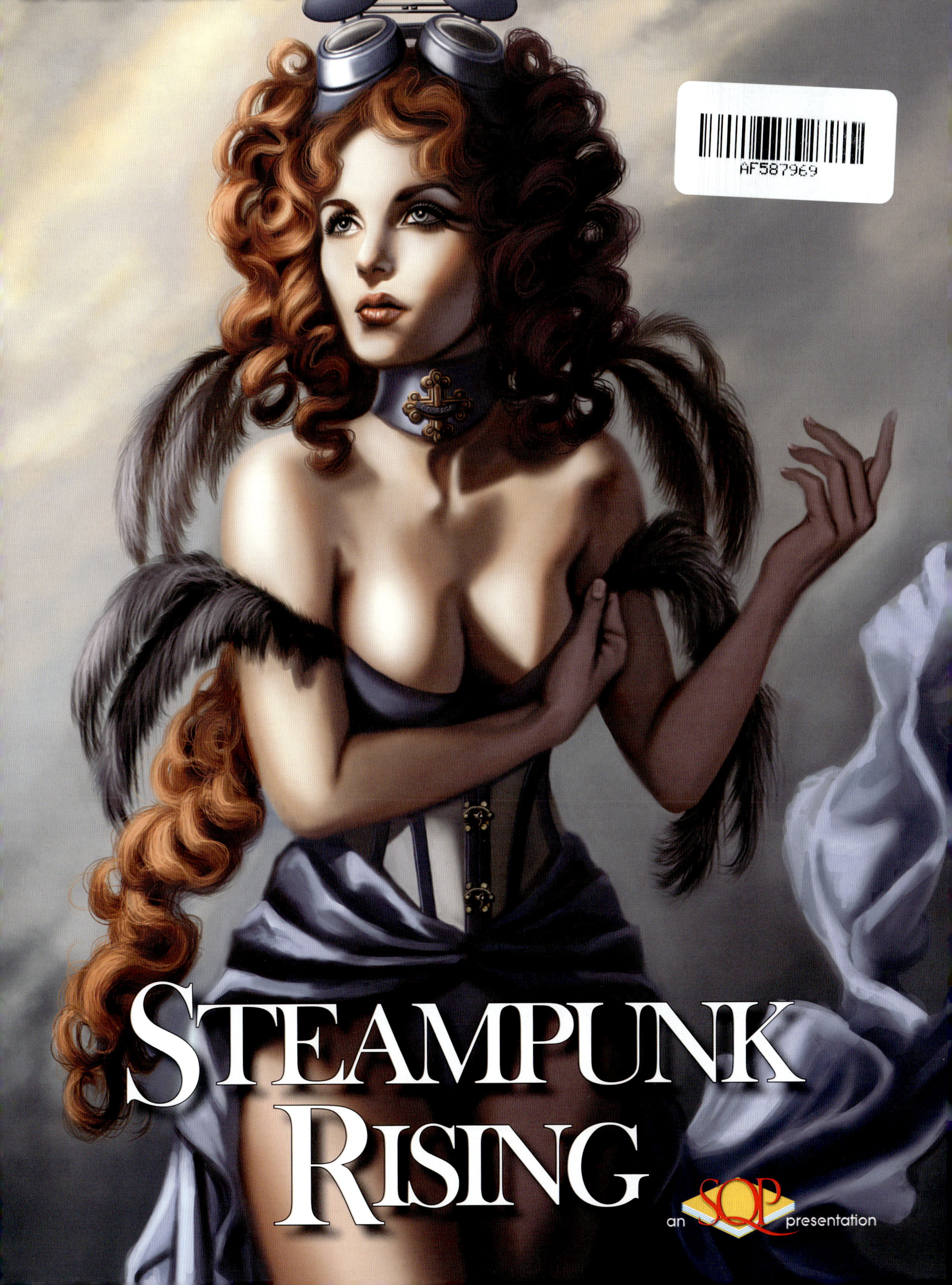

STEAMPUNK RISING

an 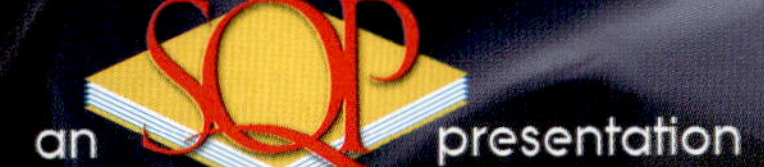 presentation

Steampunk Sirens, Gothic Geishas, and highly Flirtatious Fairies...

Artist Sandra Chang-Adair delights in creating new ways of envisioning fantasy

Sandra Chang is a self-taught artist that is passionate about delineating the beauty of the human form. She loves painting realistic fantasy and steampunk art and drawing comics. She primarily works in Photoshop, Painter, Manga Studio and Illustrator, but occasionally paints in oils. Sandra established herself in the art world by self-publishing comics in the 1990's with ***Achilles Storm*** and ***Akemi***. She has worked for ***Fantagraphics/Eros Comix***, creating and drawing X-rated comics, ***Sheedeva***, ***Sin Metal Sirens*** and contributing to Eros Anthologies. Her artwork has been published in ***Heavy Metal***, ***Erotic Signature Vols. 1-4***, ***Exotique 3***, ***Drakaina Masters***, ***Infected by Art, Vols. 1 & 2*** and the ***Michael Jackson Opus Book***. She has done CCG cards for ***Vampire of the Masquerade*** and ***Alderac Entertainment***. She has extensive magazine work, illustrated pin-ups for ***Hustler Magazine*** regularly from 2009 - 2012 and was the staff artist and painted editorial articles for ***Inside Kung Fu Magazine*** from 2003 - 2007. She has written numerous tutorials for ***Fantasy Art Magazine***, ***Digital Artist Magazine***, ***Corel Painter Magazine*** and ***Advanced Photoshop Magazine***. You can view more of Sandra's art on her website, **www.sandrachang.net** and purchase exclusive, handmade jewelry with her art and signed prints at **www.etsy.com/shop/steampunkfantasyart.**

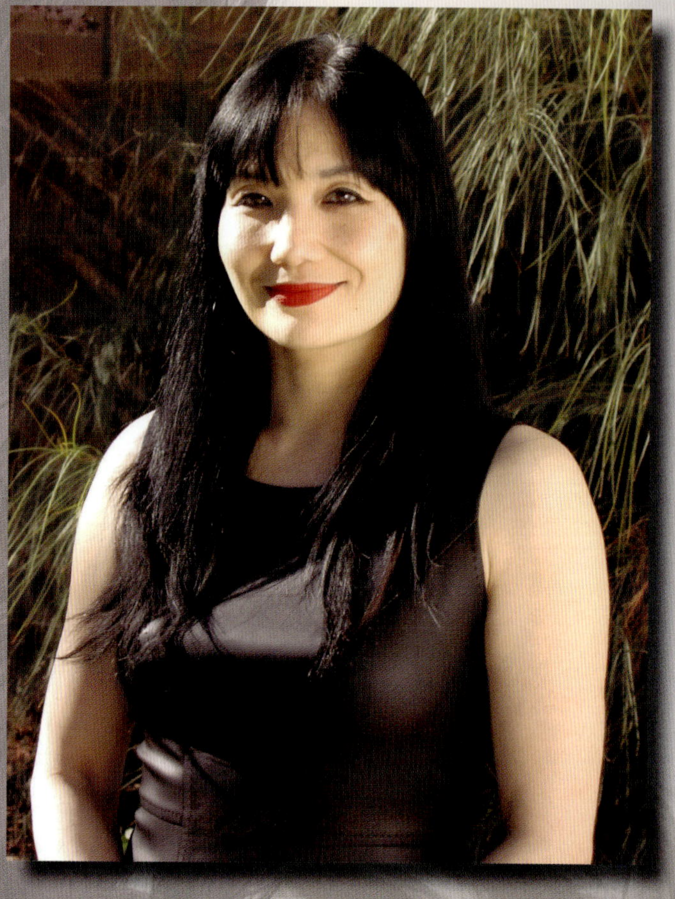

Sandra is currently returning to the world of comics and working on her online comic called ***Gothic Geisha***, a sci-fi/martial arts story set in a future dystopia (visit **www.gothicgeisha.com**). She has developed her own **Female Empowerment Brand** of cartoon characters called ***Banzai Chicks*** (**www.banzaichicks.com**) and currently sells handmade jewelry with these cute, Kawaii style characters at **www.etsy.com/shop/banzaichicks.**

Sandra also enjoys writing, graphic design, canine freestyle and dog agility. Her main passion besides art is practicing martial arts. She has a 2nd degree blackbelt in Budoshin Ju Jitsu, a 1st degree black sash in Northern Eagle Claw and certificates in Traditional Kung Fu and Traditional Weapons. She is currently a student at Shaolin Kung Fu Chan, a school run by Shi Xing Wei, a 32nd generation Shaolin Monk from China. She also trains at Shaolin Tai Chi Cultural Center with Shi Chang Yuan, a 33rd generation Shaolin Monk. Sandra lives in Las Vegas, Nevada with her husband, Dustin Adair, a mobile phone game developer and her dogs, Ripley and Freckles.

Steampunk Rising
The Art of Sandra Chang-Adair

Book design by Grassy Knoll Studios.

Published by SQP Inc.
PO Box 248 - Columbus NJ 08022

Sal Quartuccio & Bob Keenan - Publishers

For a free, full color catalog showcasing the entire SQP line of erotic, fantasy, and pin-up artwork, go to:
www.sqpartbooks.com

Since 1973, showcasing the very finest in fantasy, erotic, & pin-up illustration.

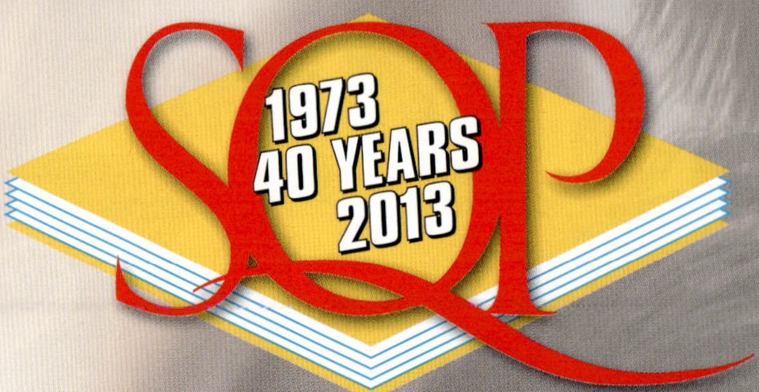

www.sqpartbooks.com

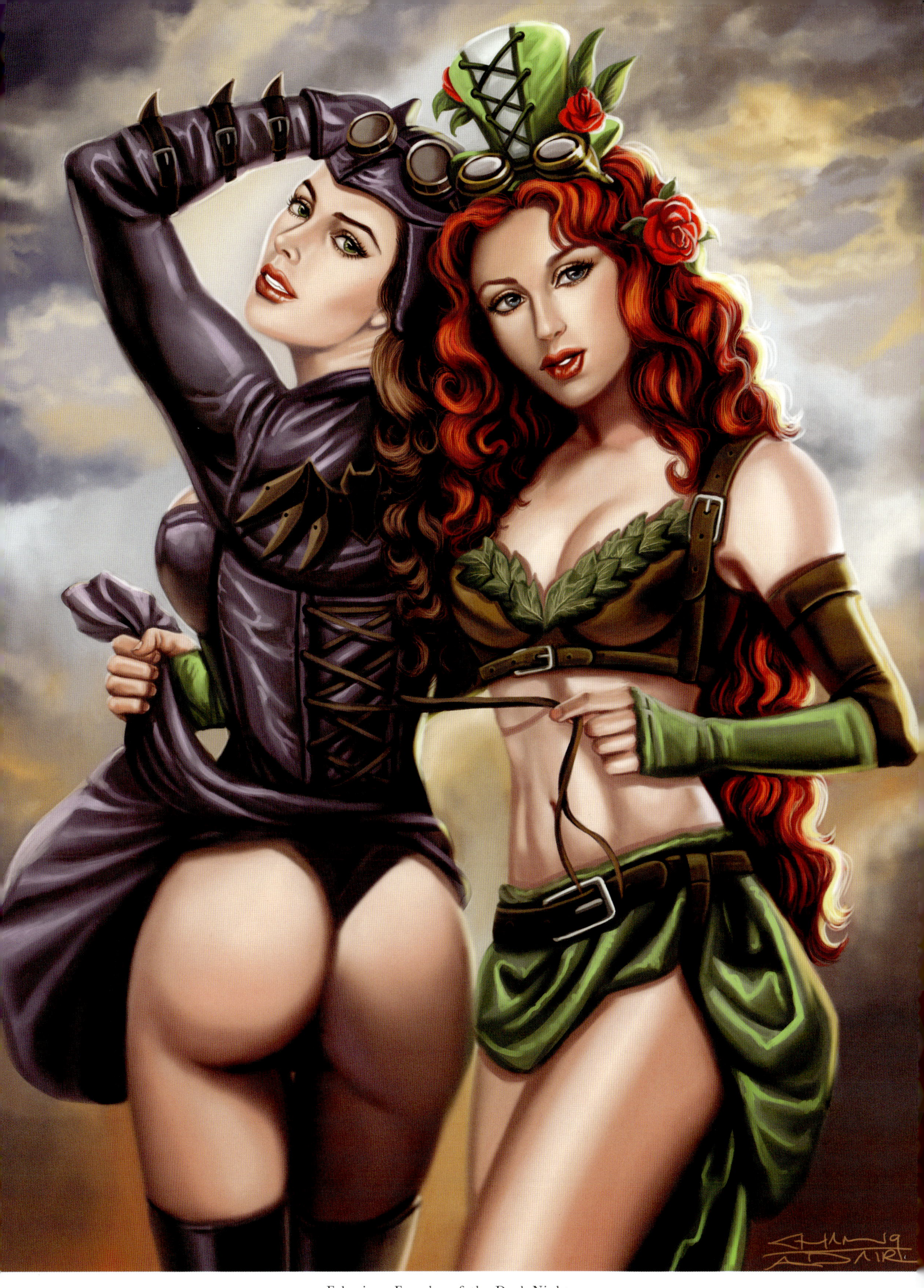

Felonious Females of the Dark Night

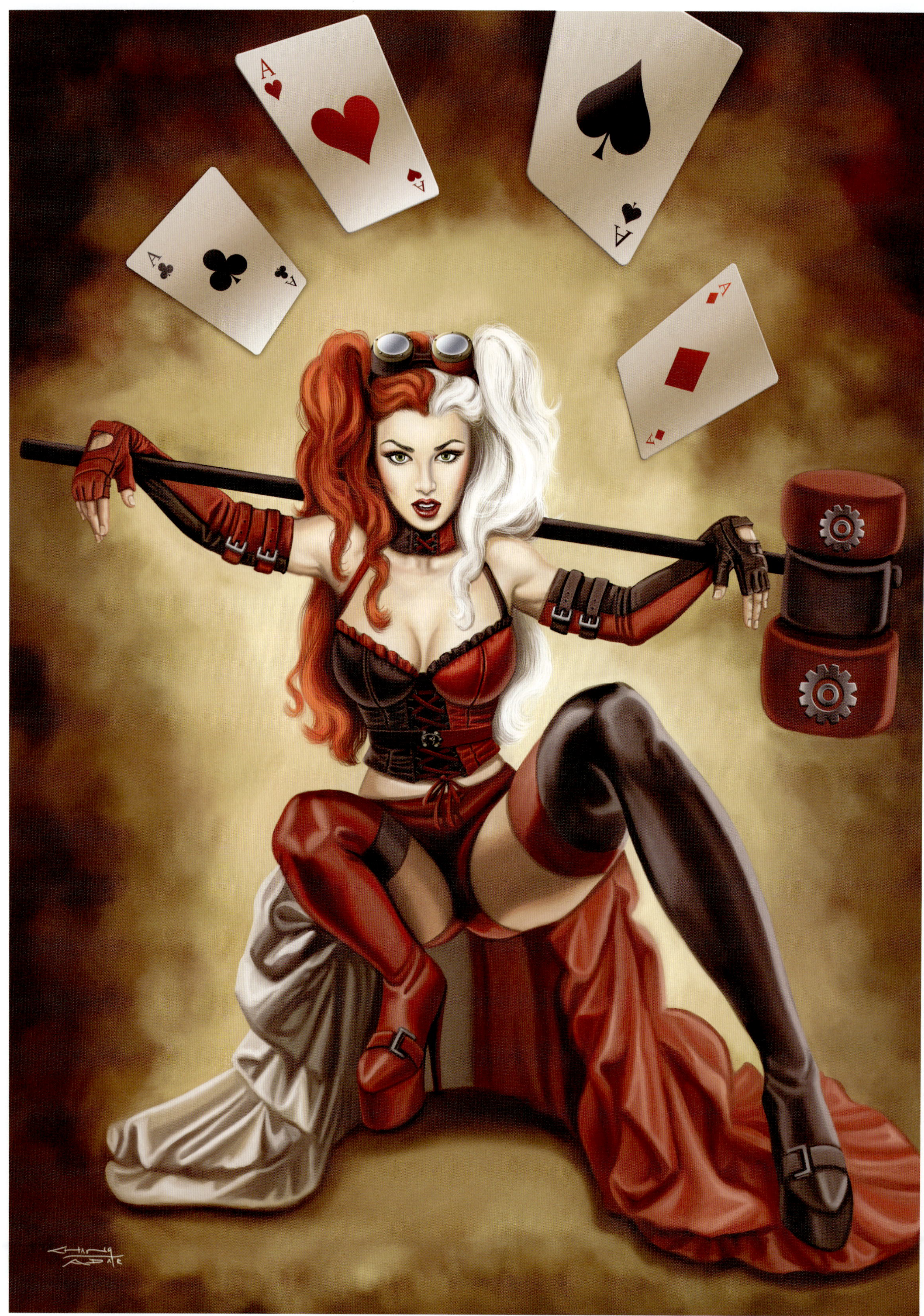

Wildest Card in the Deck

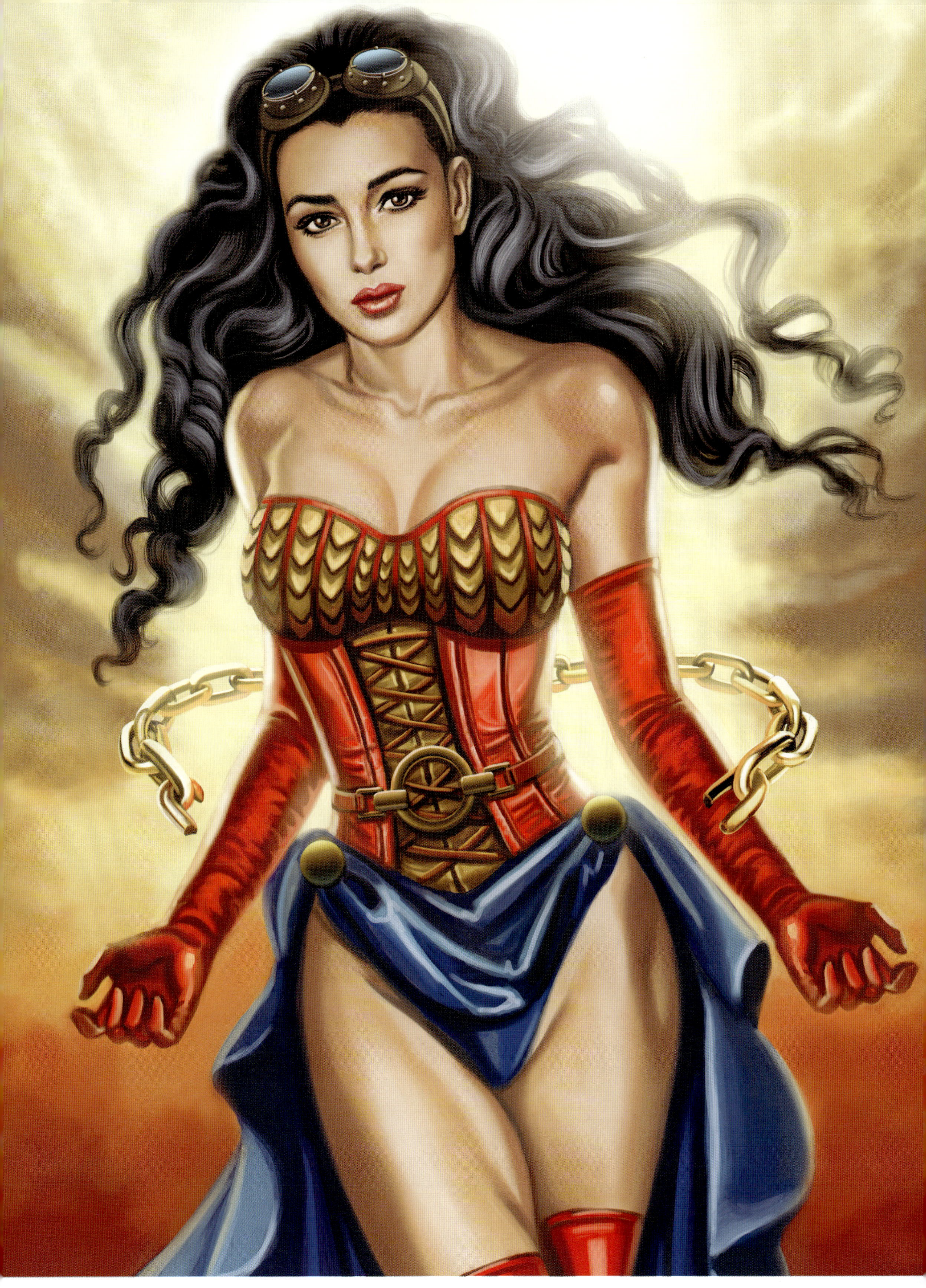

Paradise Unbound

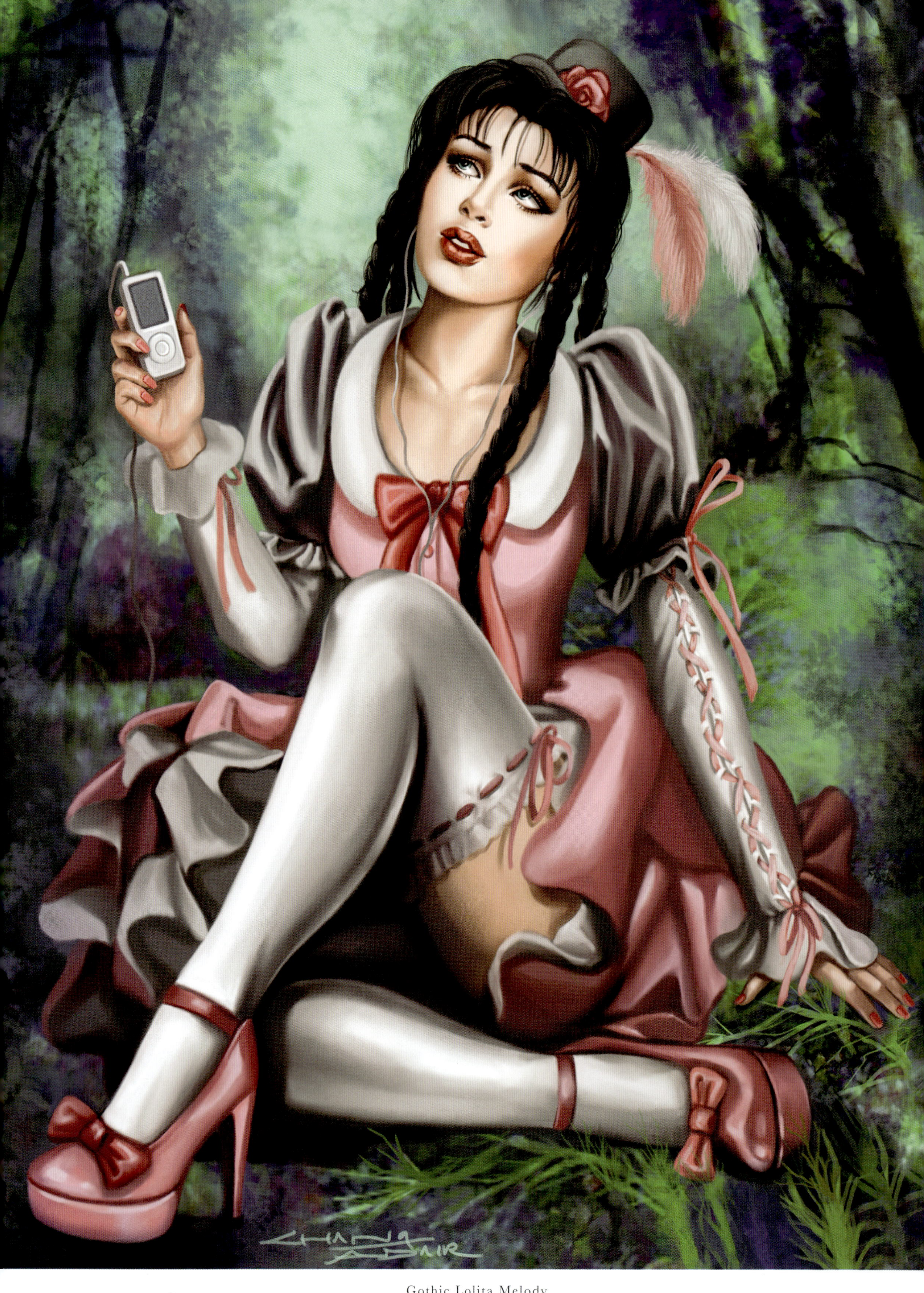

Gothic Lolita Melody

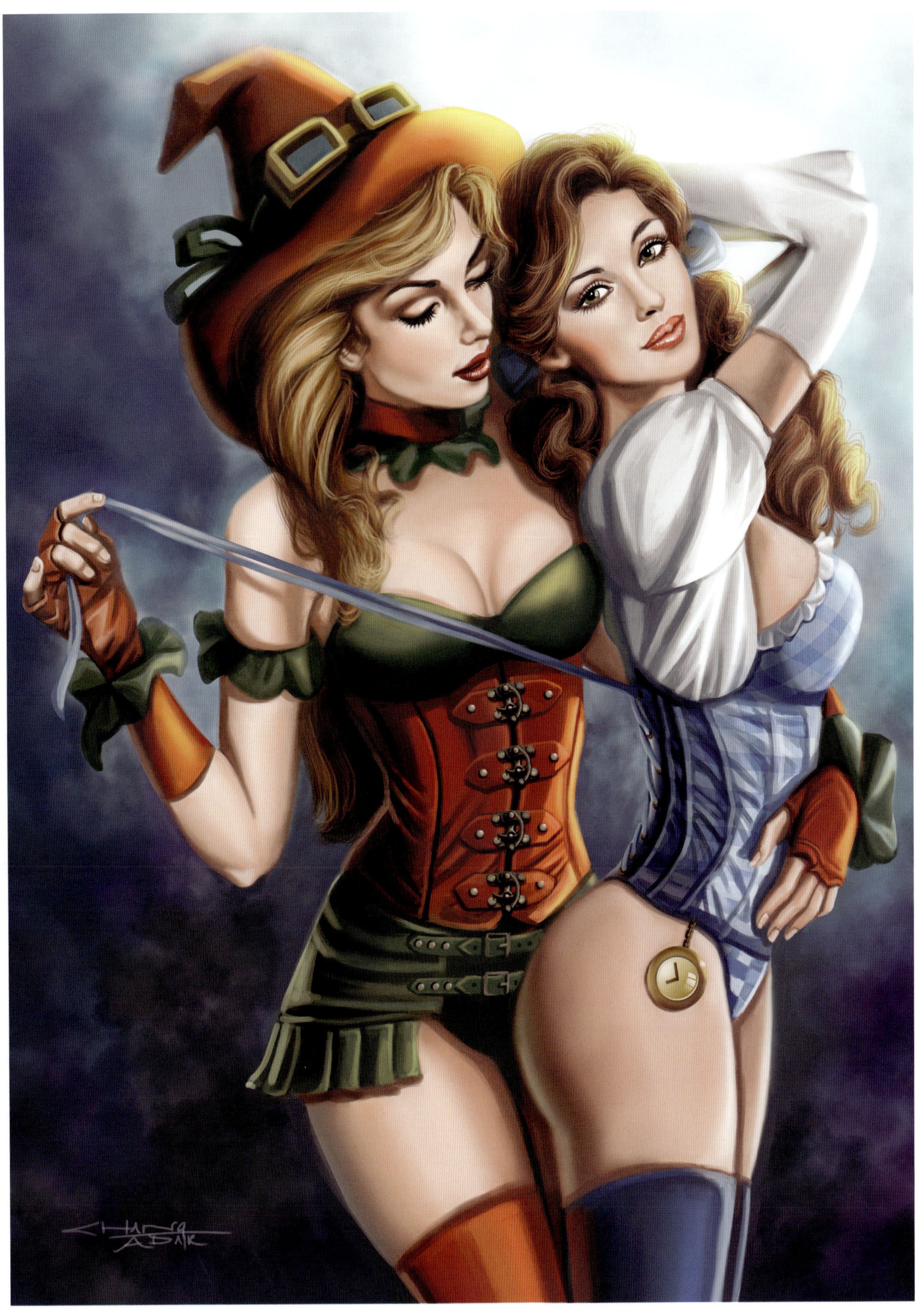

There's No Place Like Home

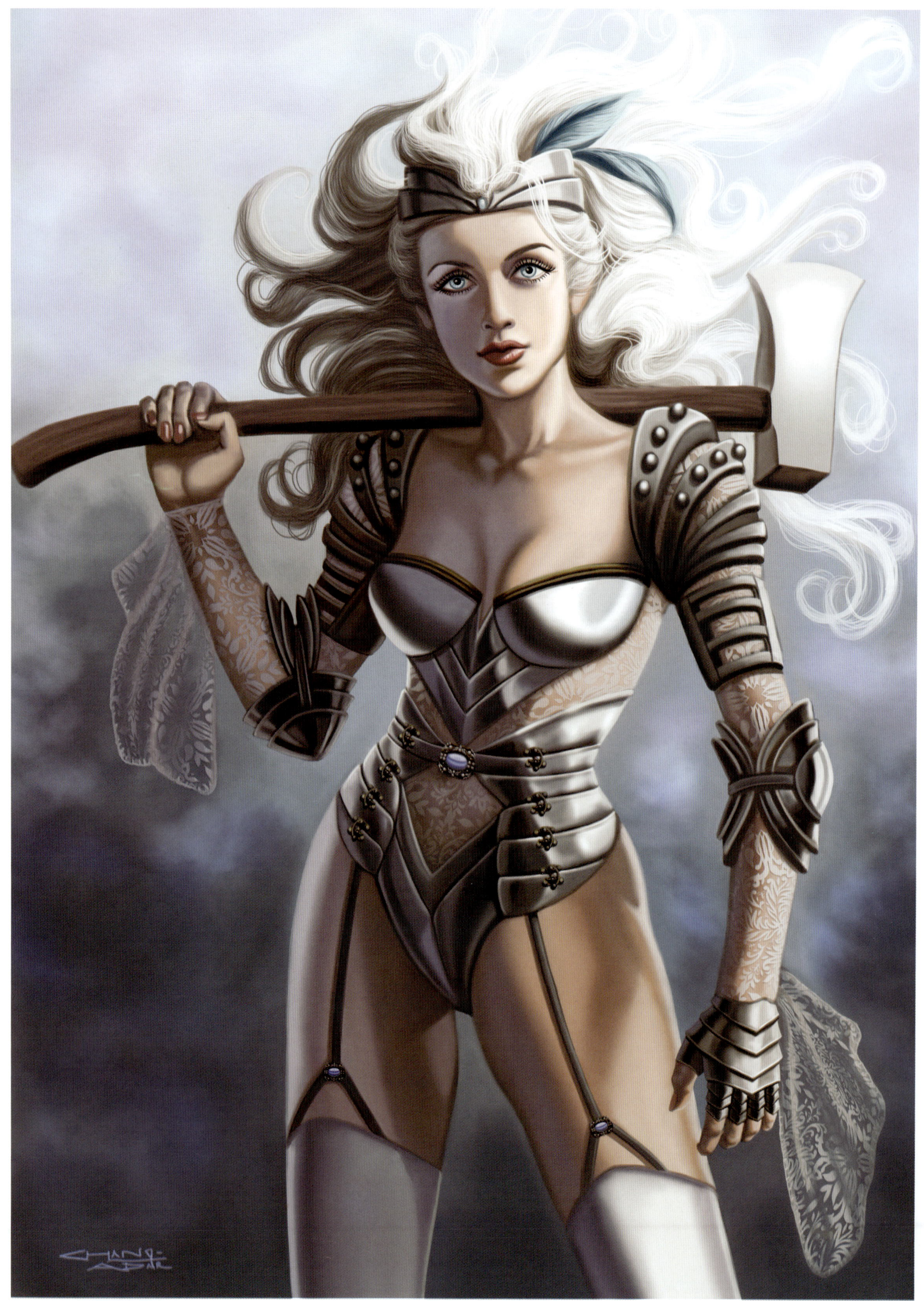

Lady Tinsmith

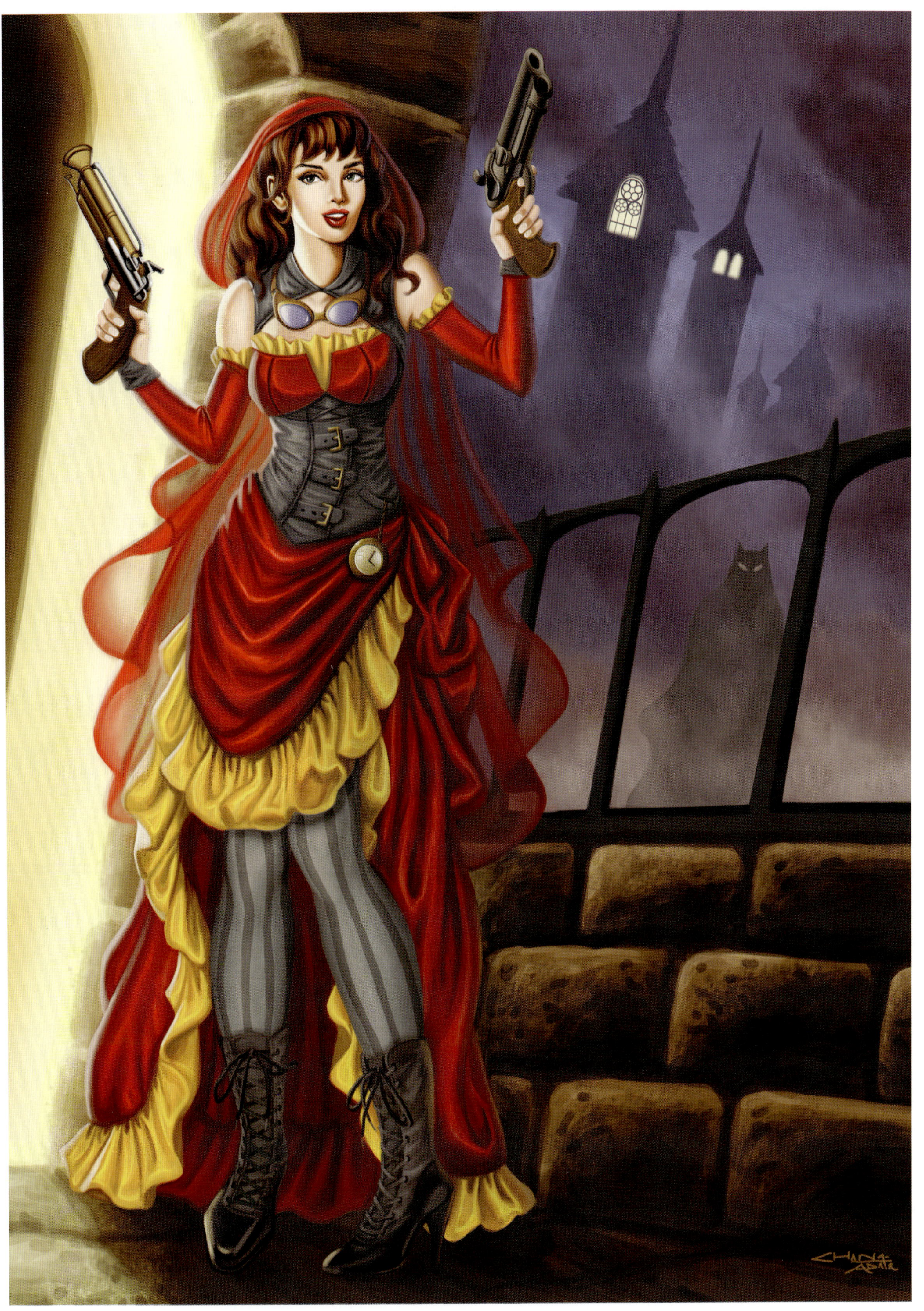

Red Riding Hood Armed & Ready

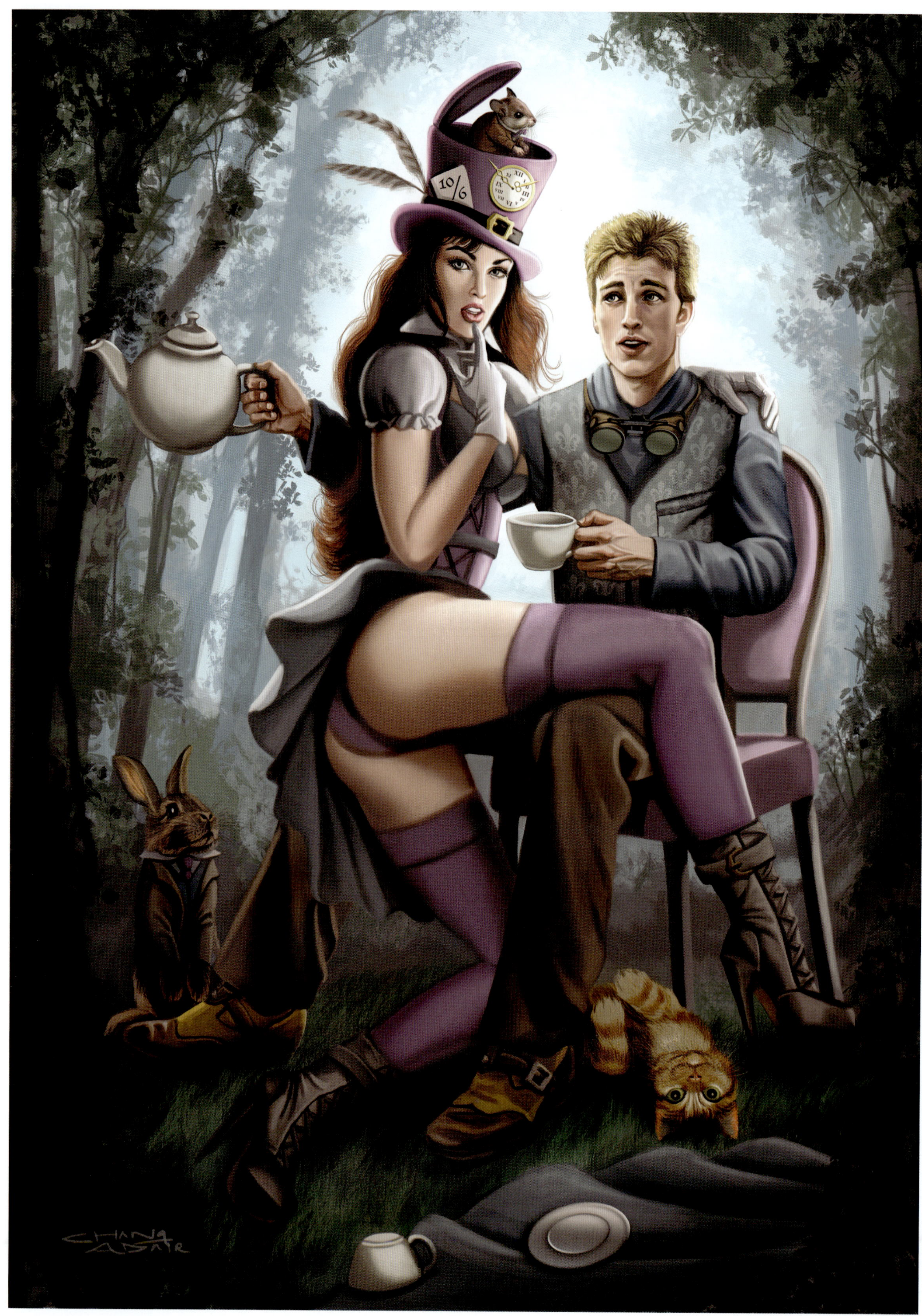

The Seduction of Alex In Wonderland

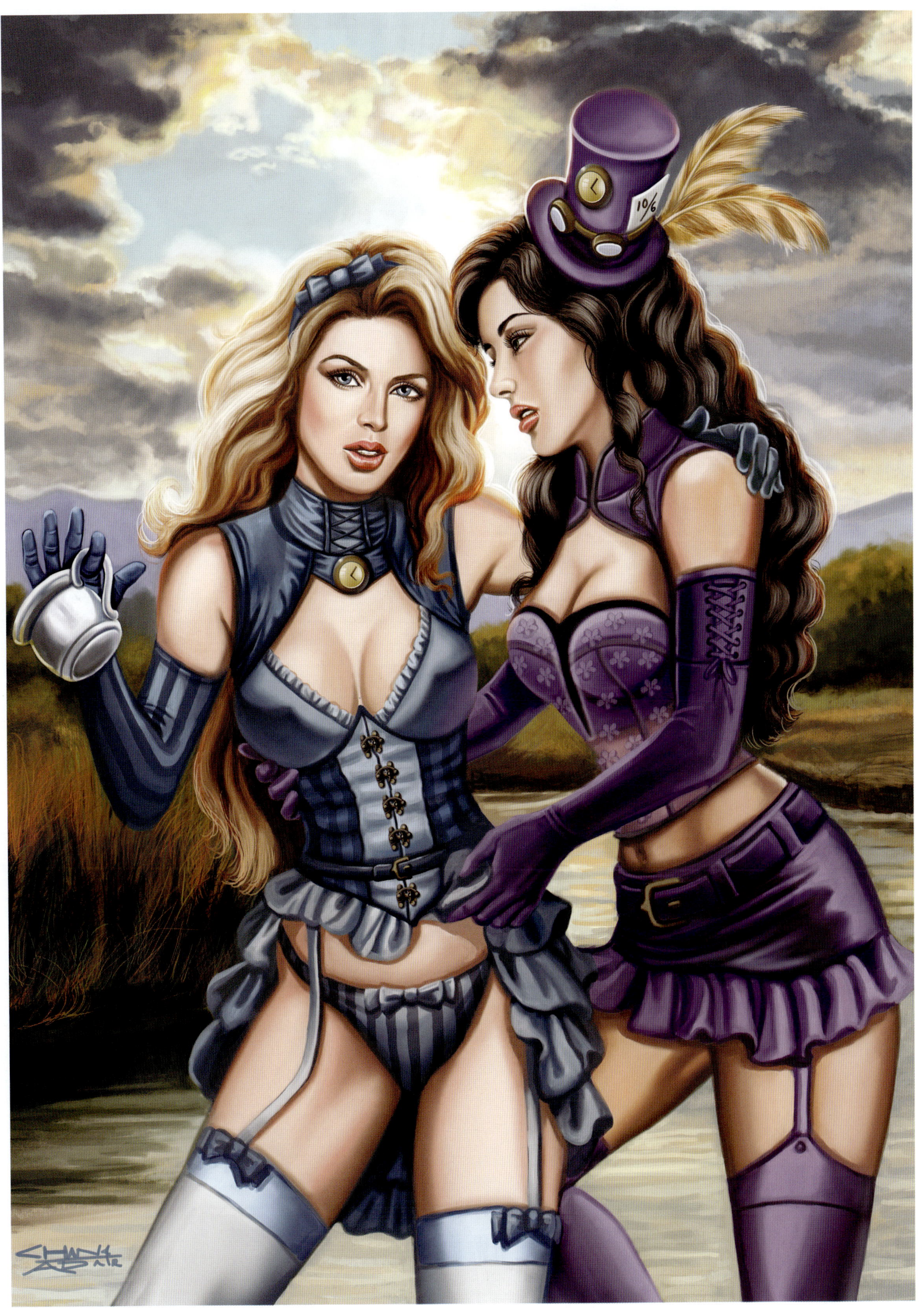

Wanderlust in Wonderland

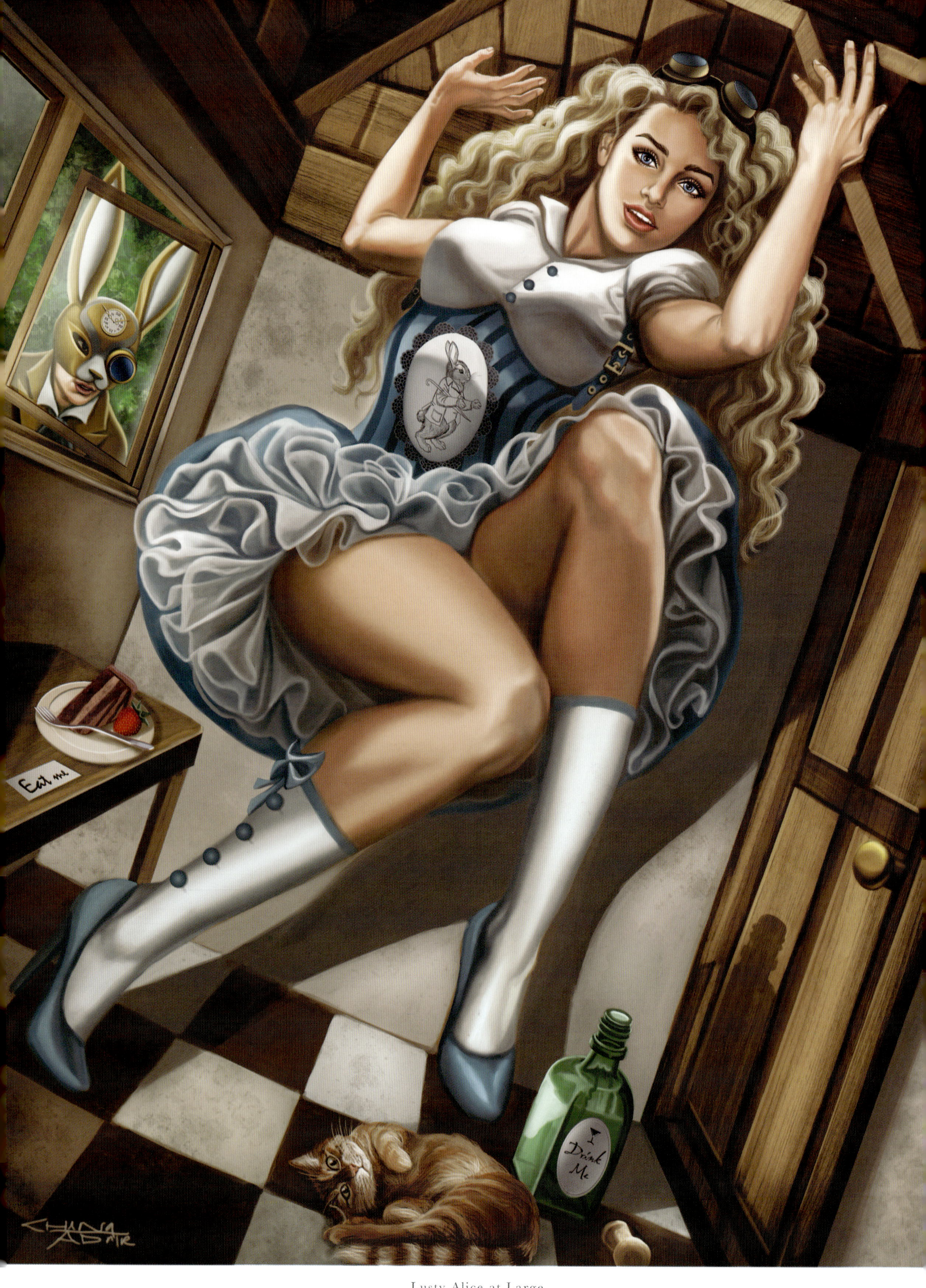

Lusty Alice at Large

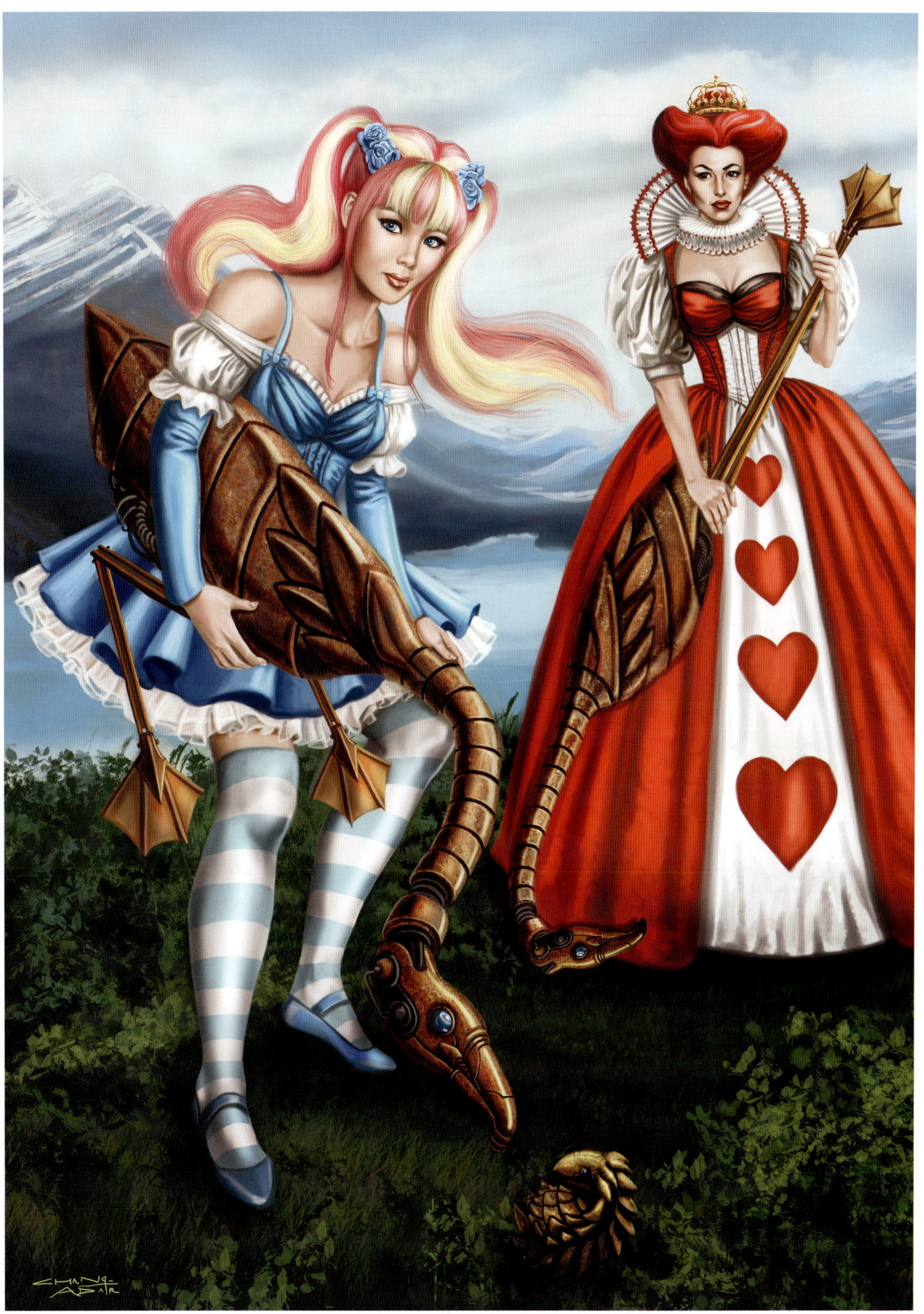

Provacative Croquet

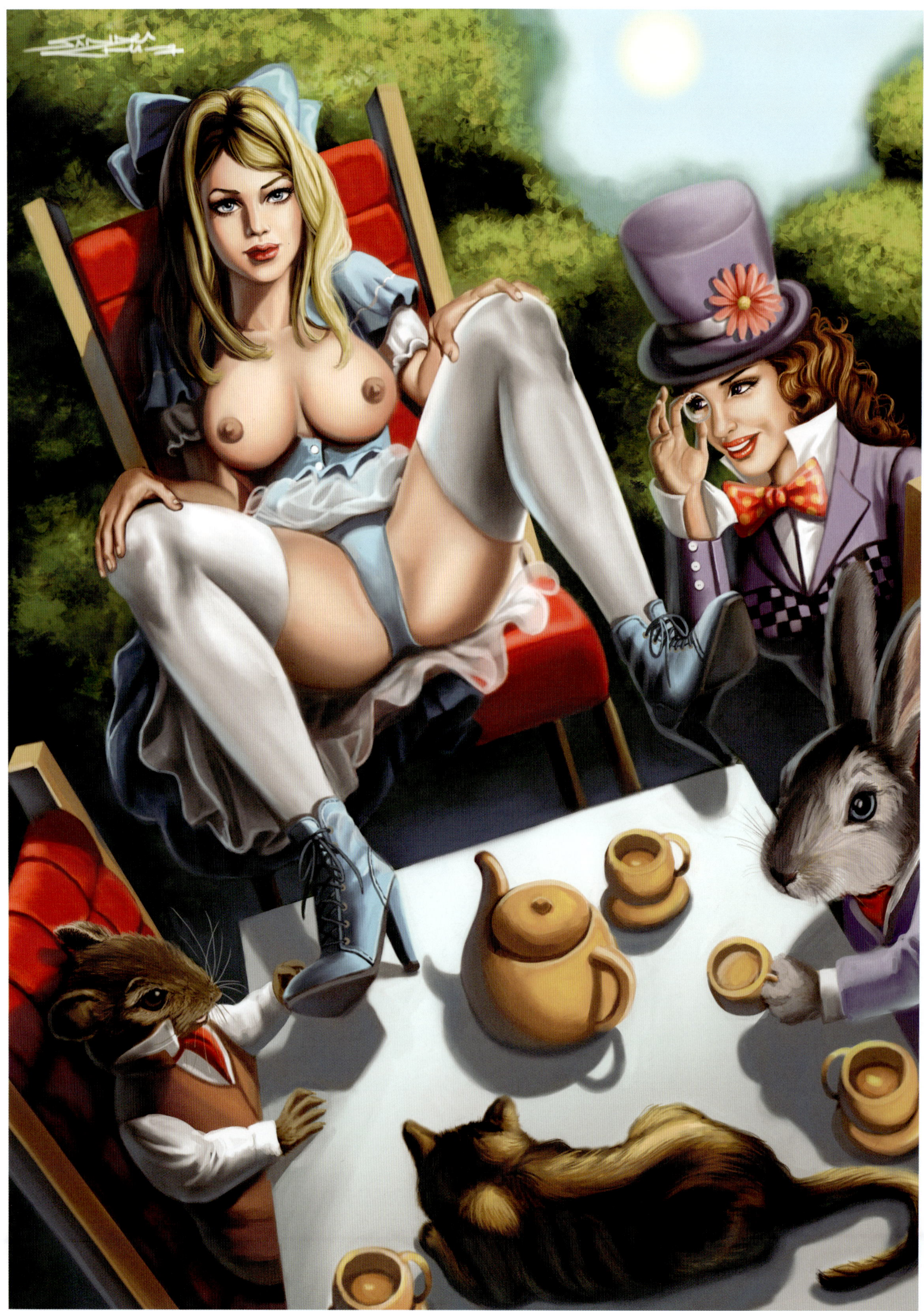

Tea Party Temptress

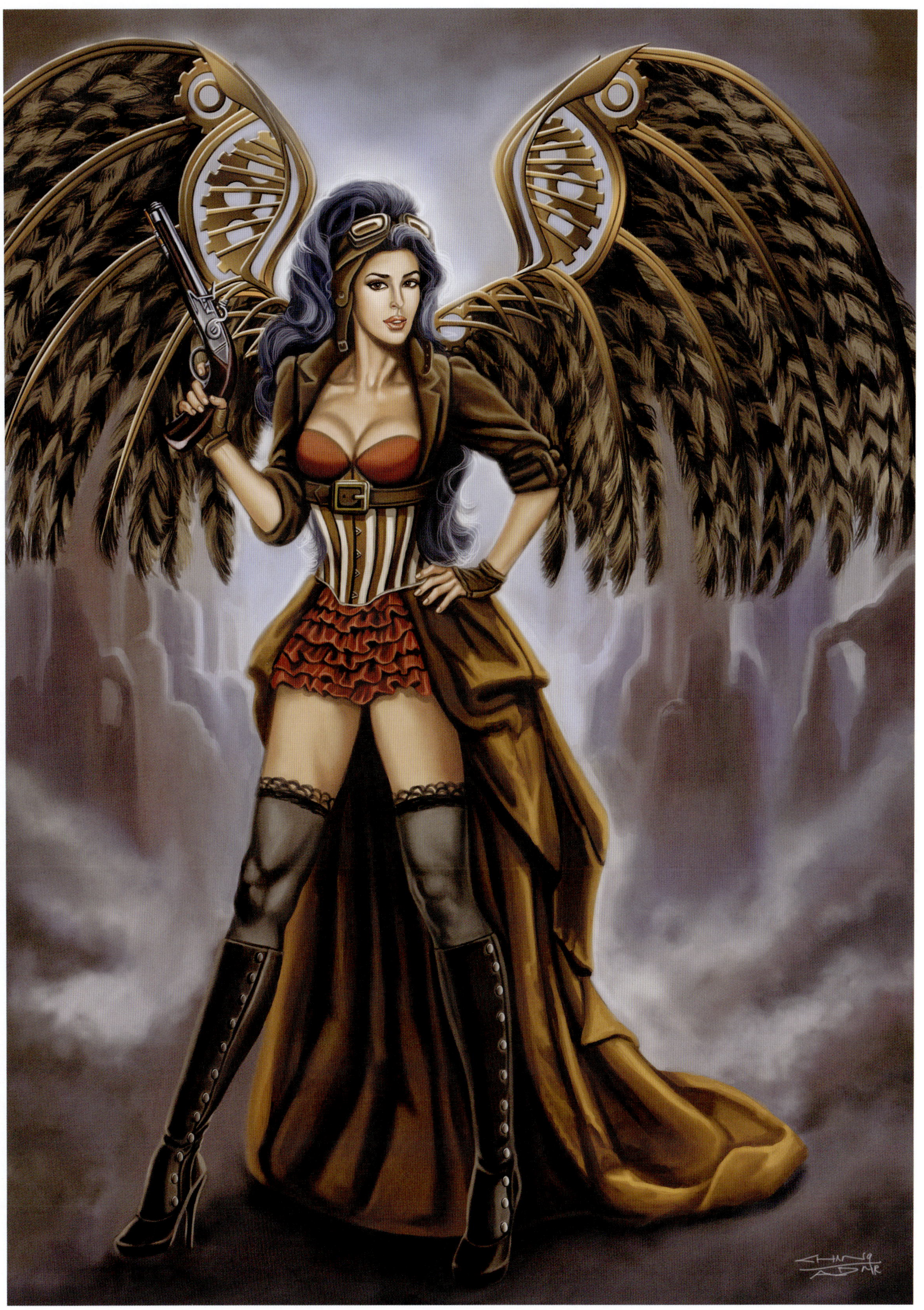

Aviatrix Extraordinare

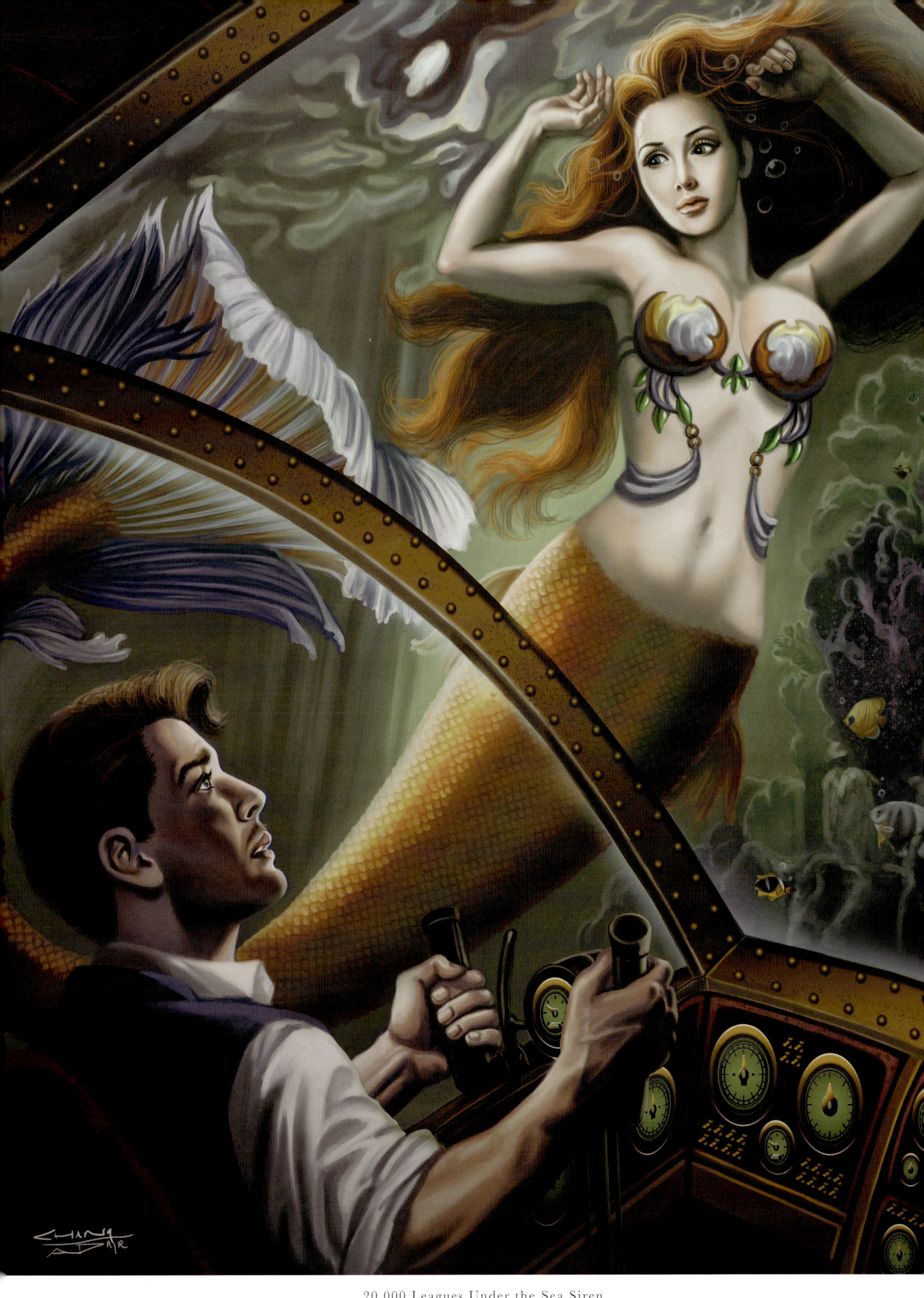

20,000 Leagues Under the Sea Siren

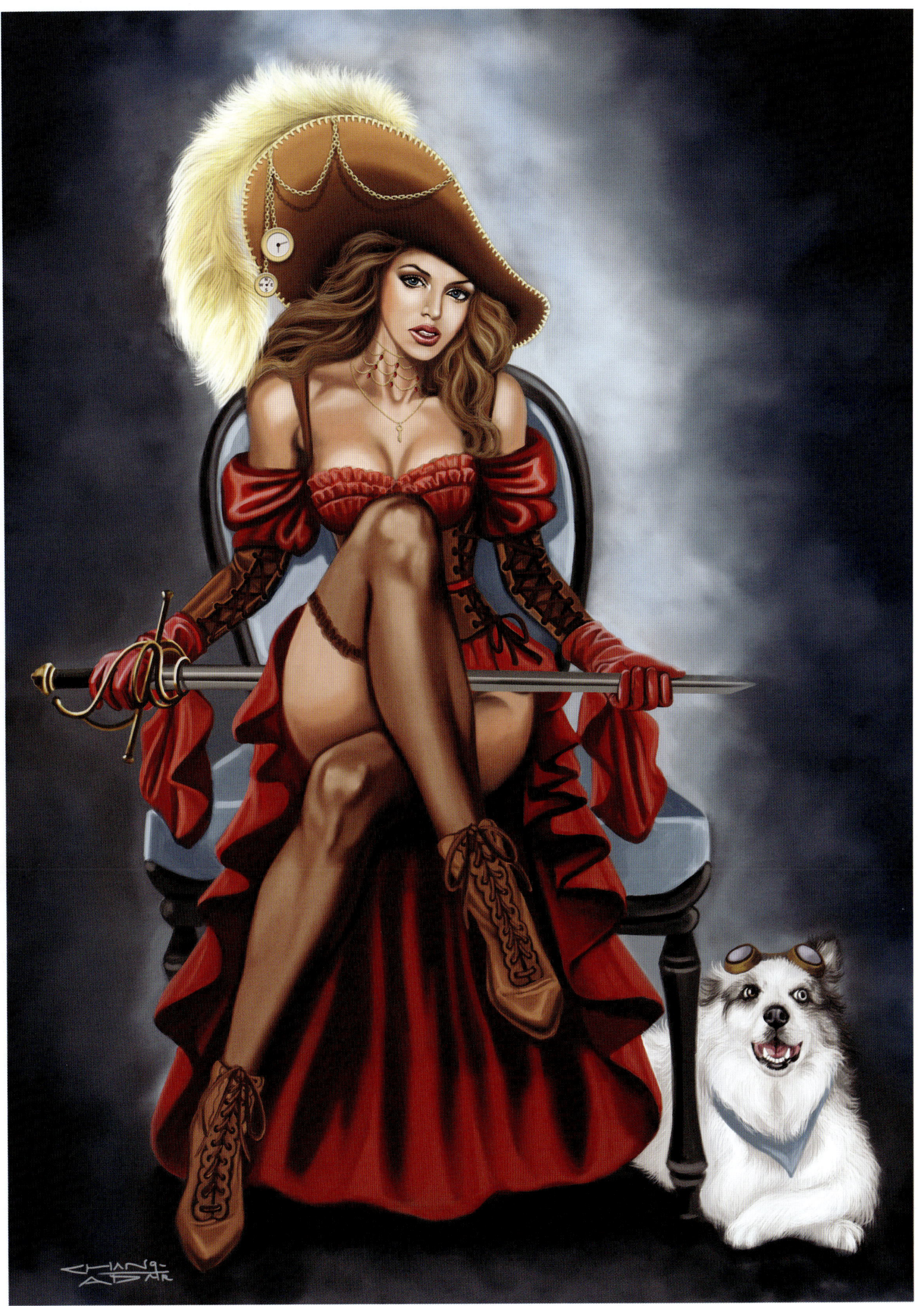

Missketeer Mistress

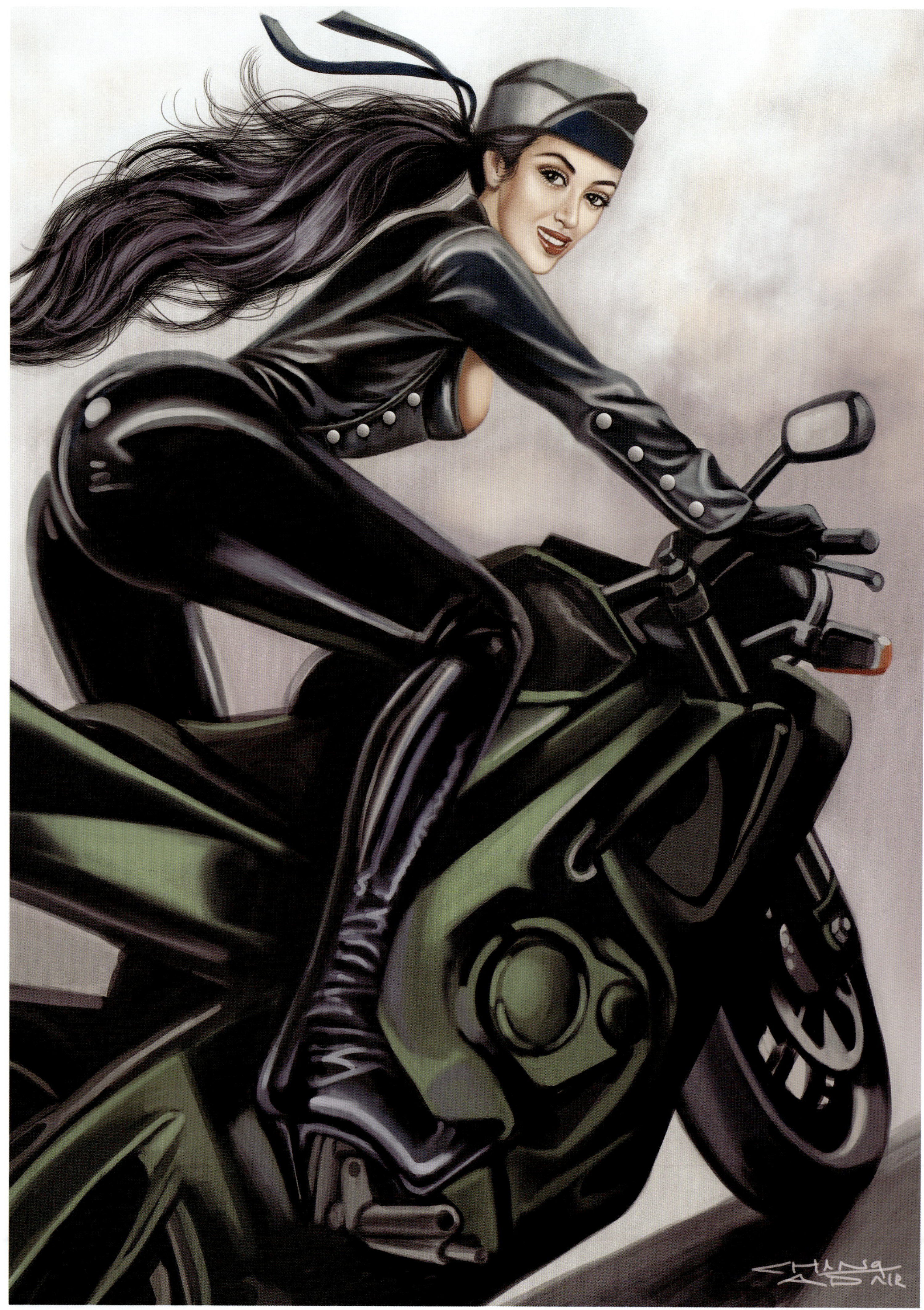

Vixen on Wheels

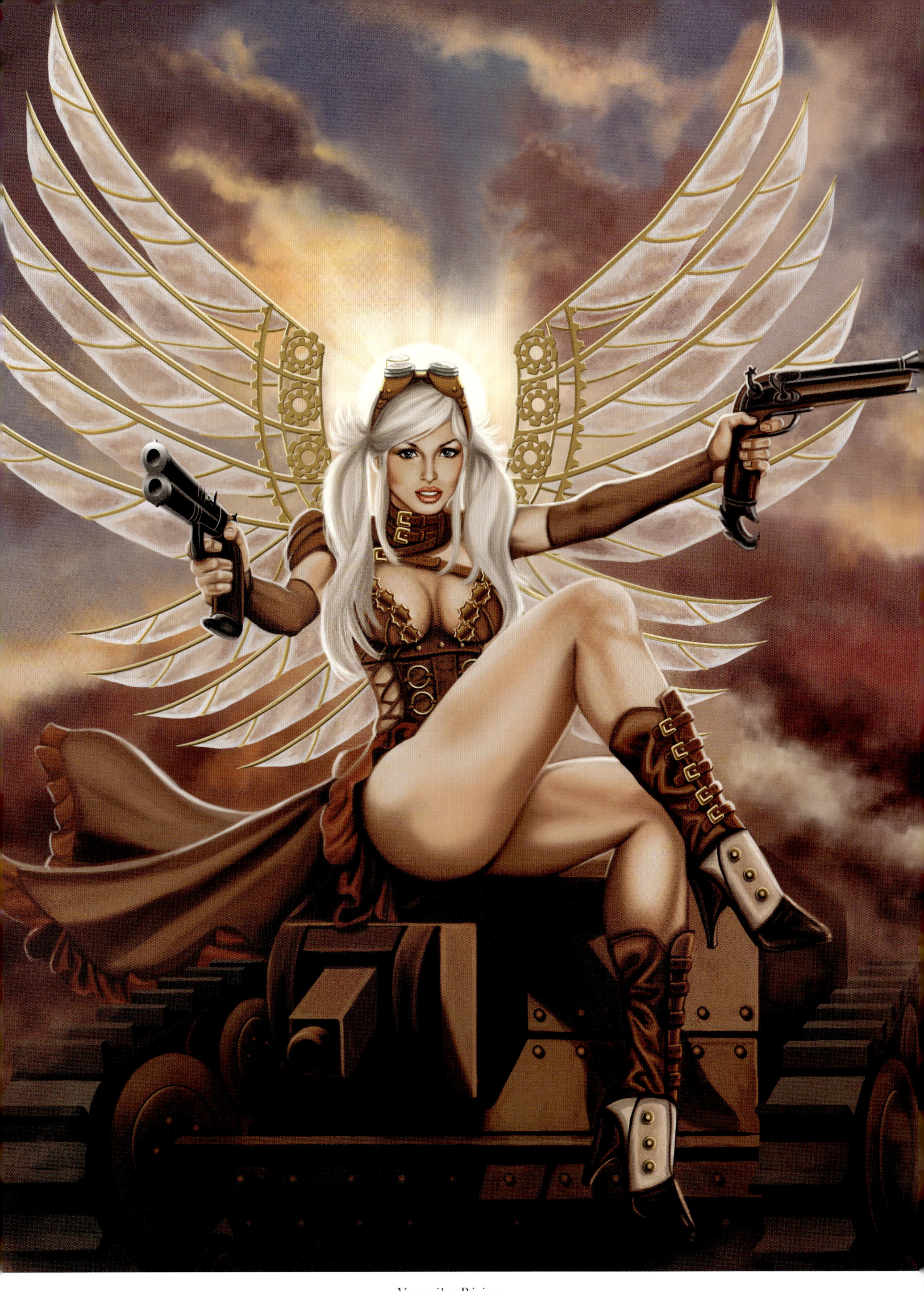

Veronika Rising

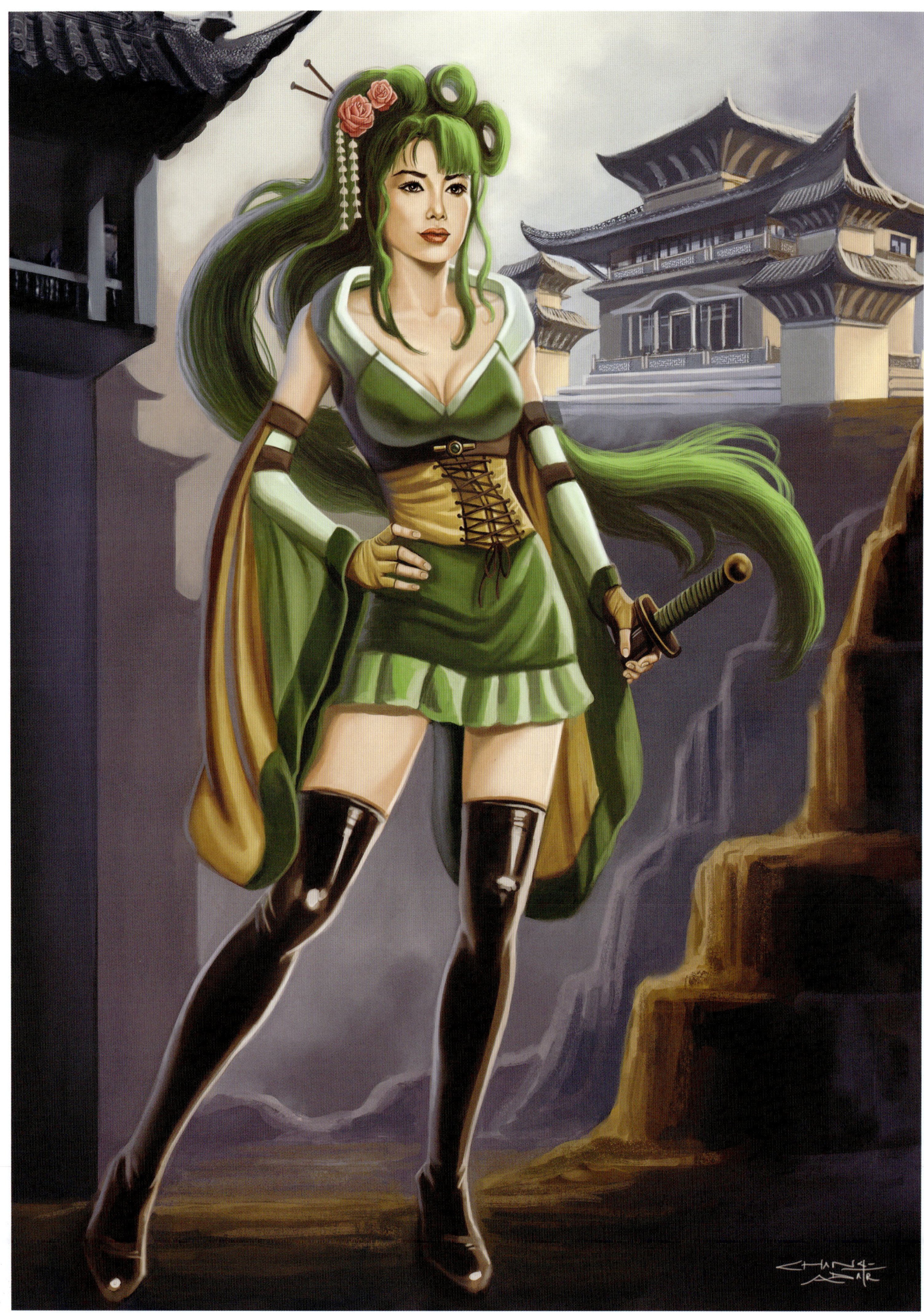

Jade Geisha in Tokyo

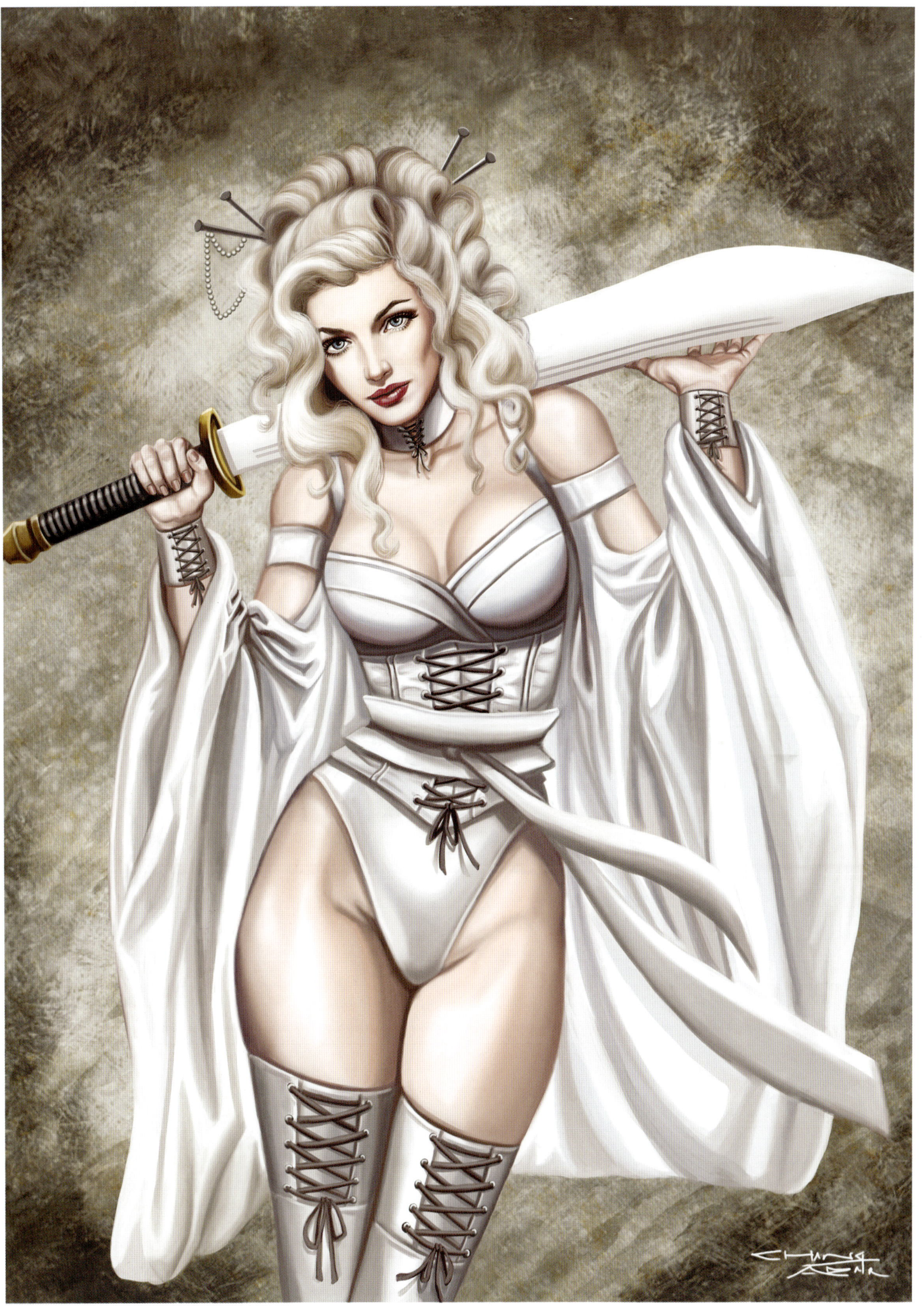

Snow Geisha

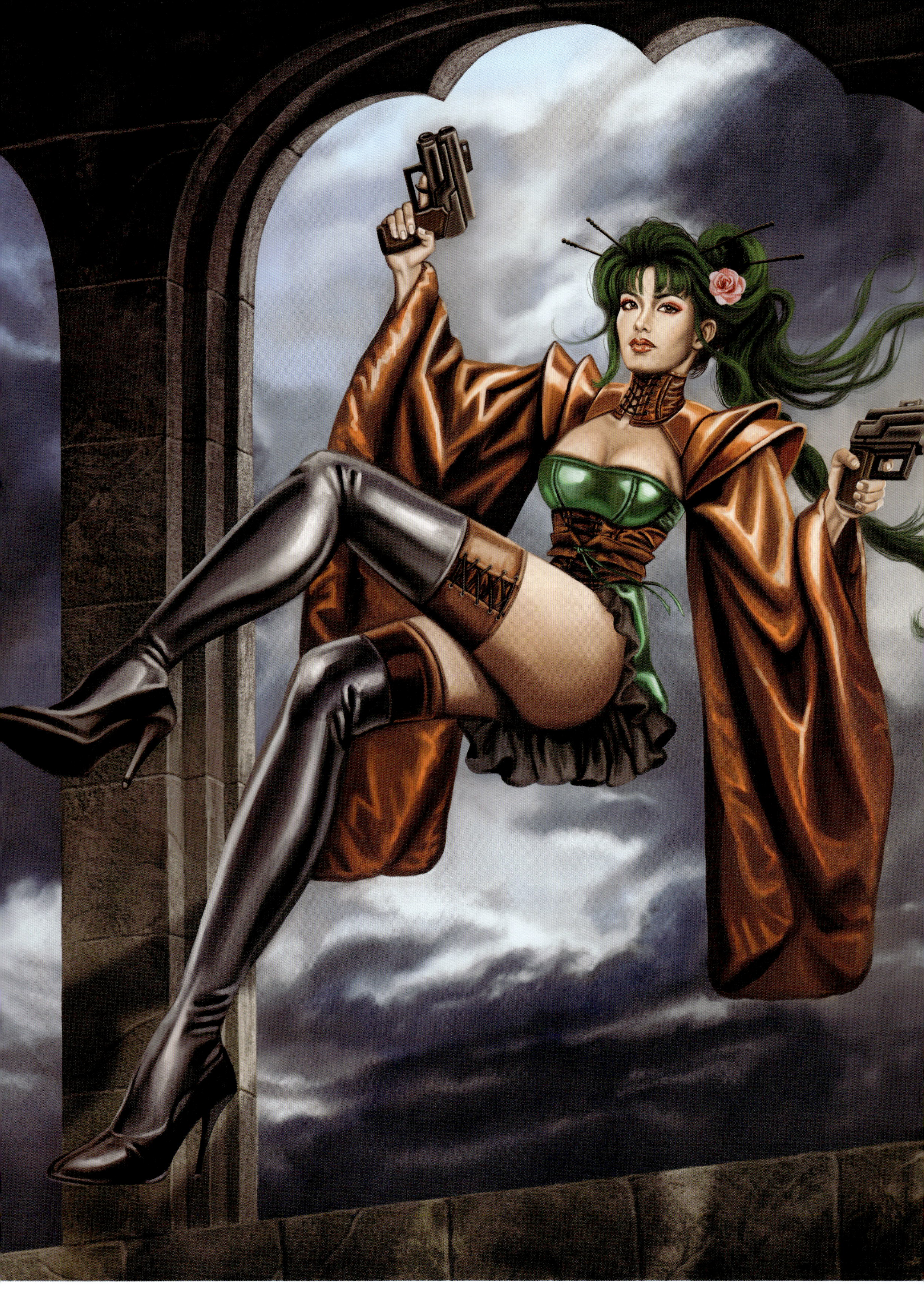

Akemi Unleashed

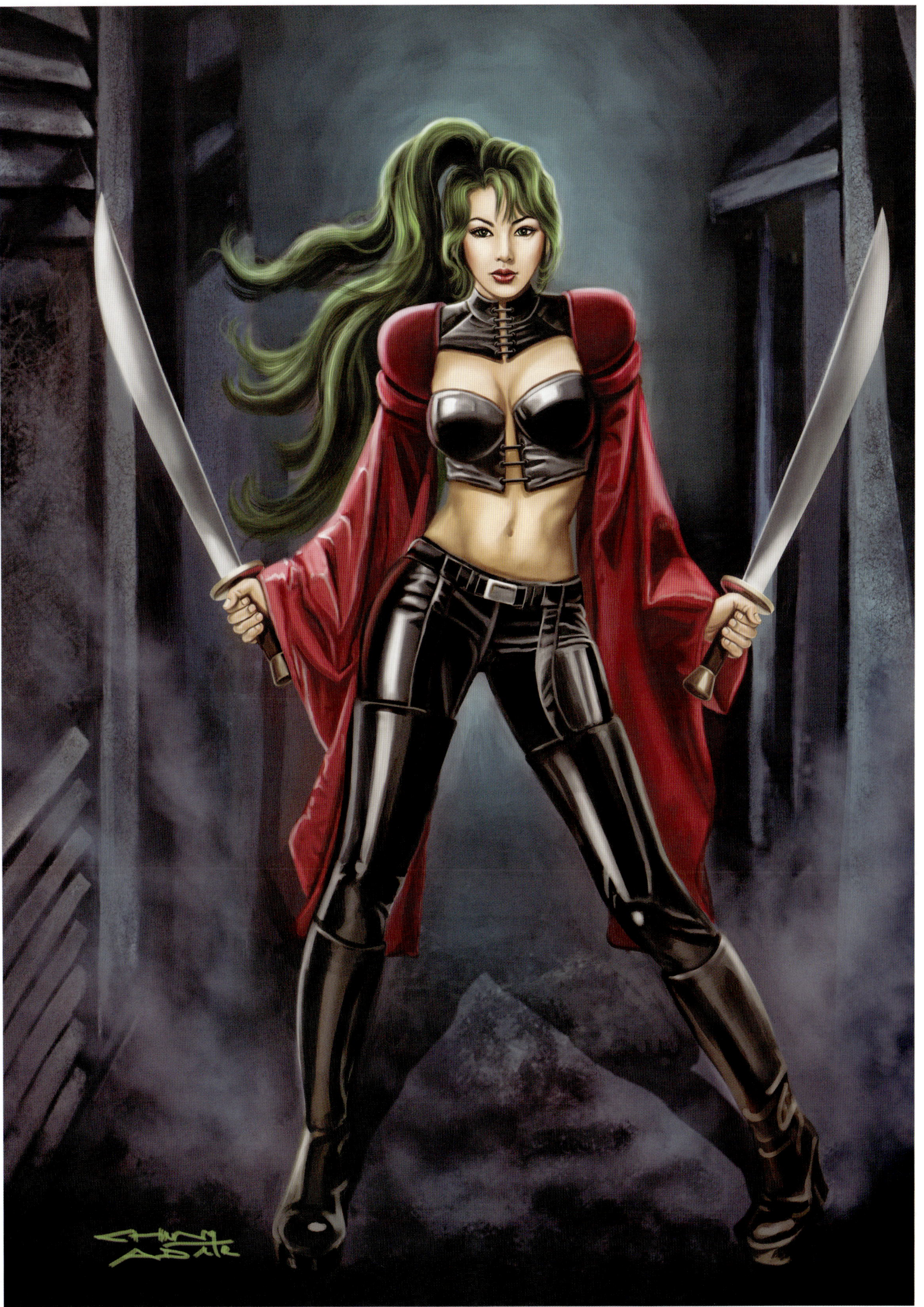

Double Sword Siren

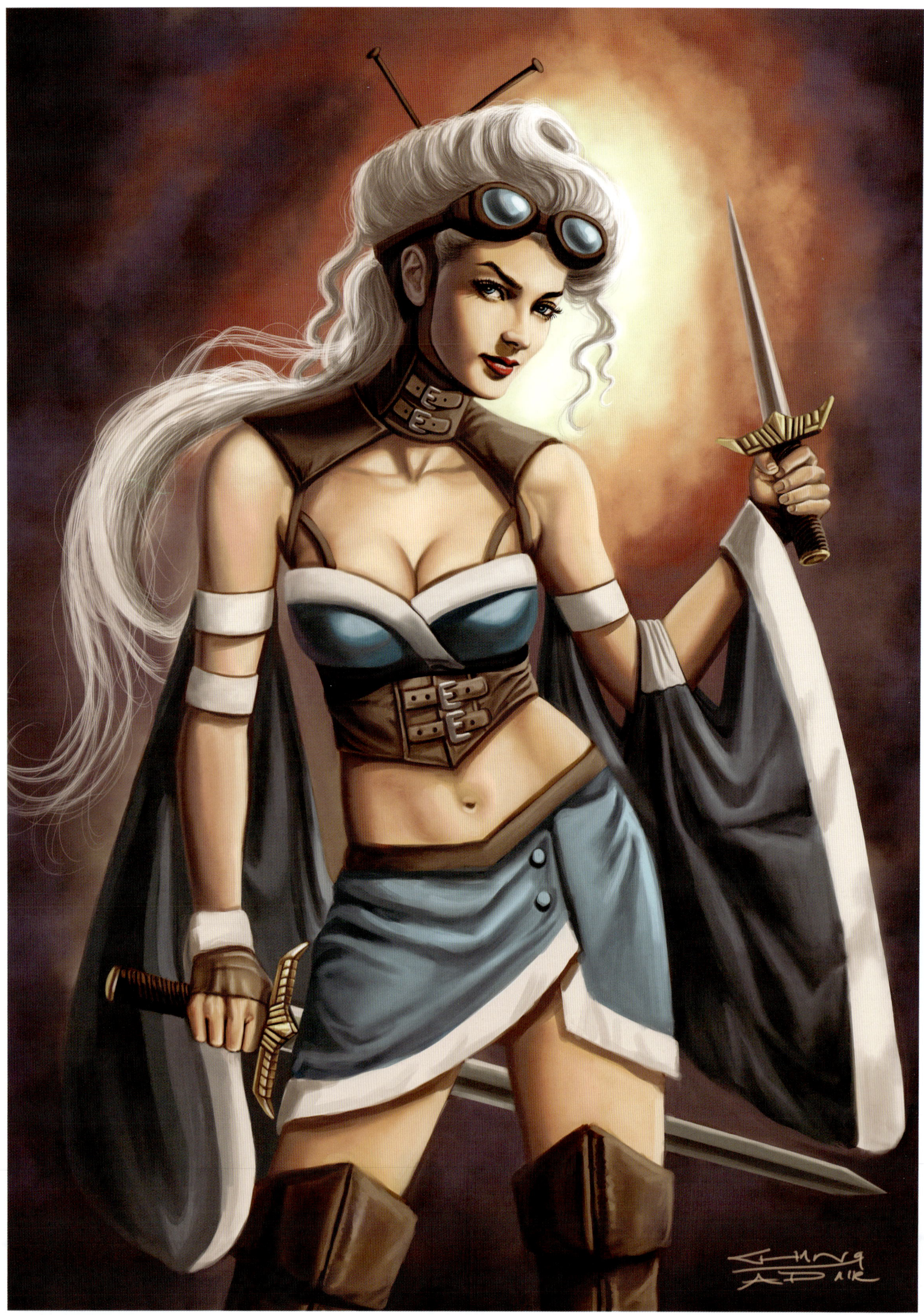

Steampunk Sasha's Swords

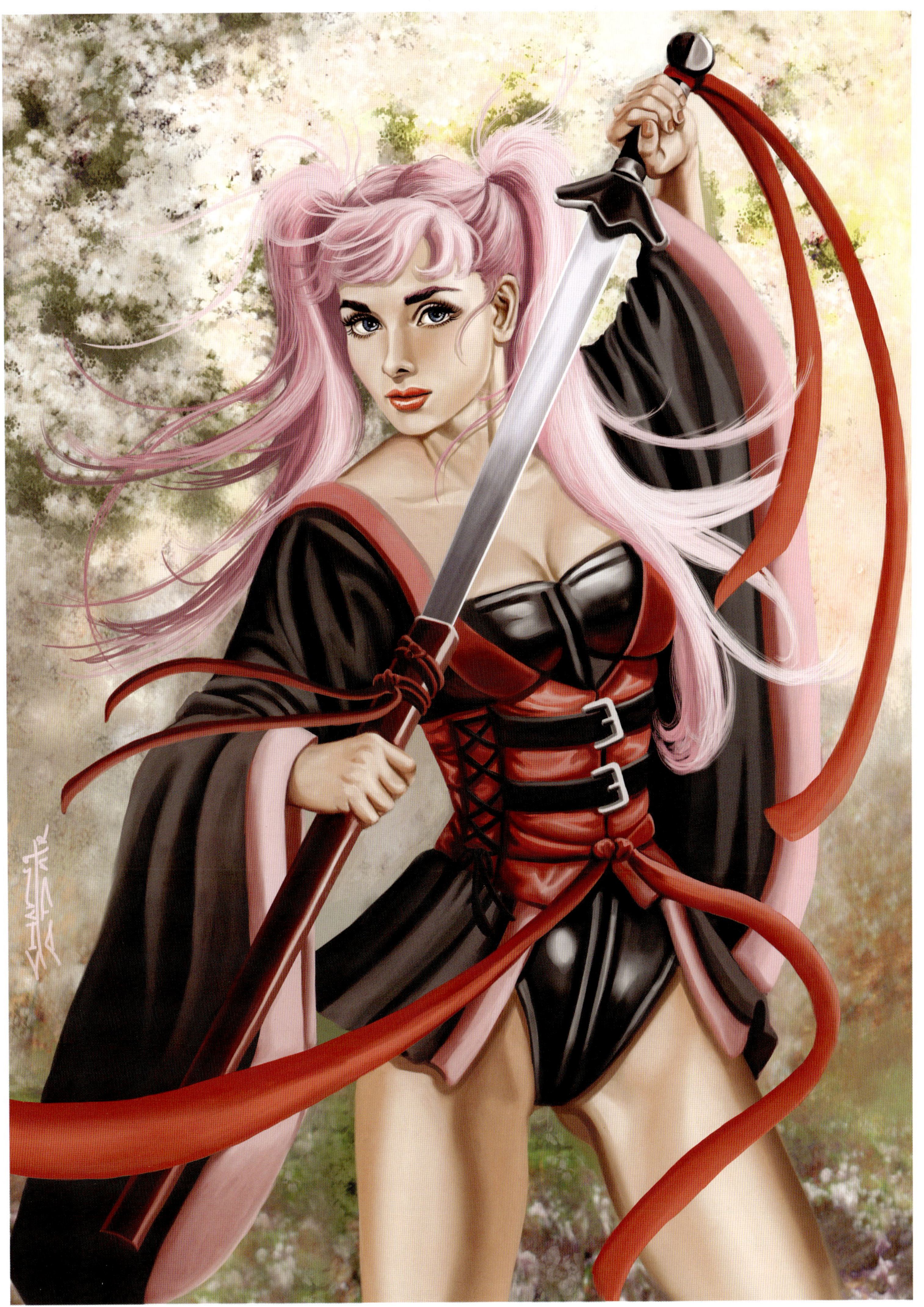

Cotton Candy Chloe

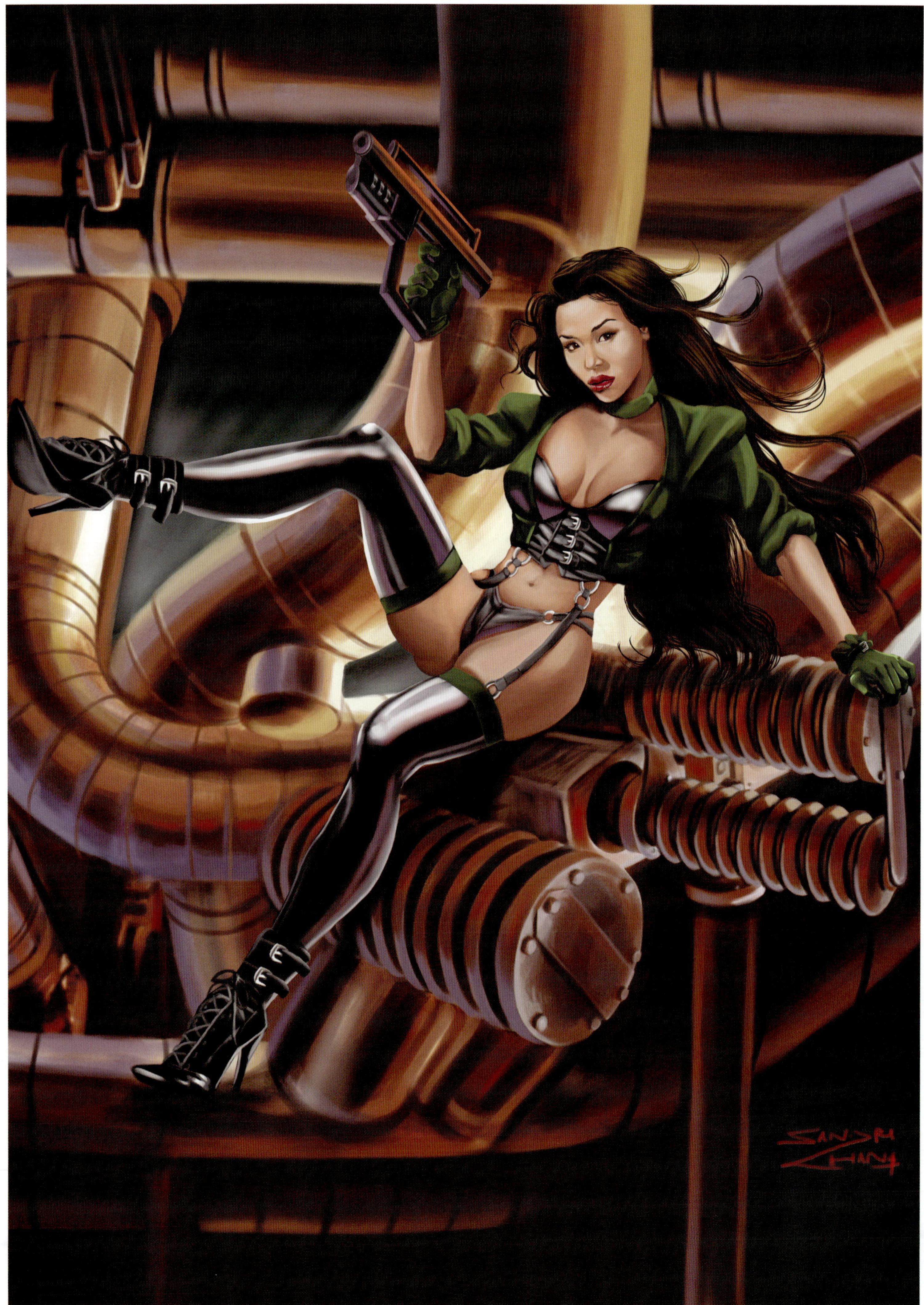

Latex and Guns

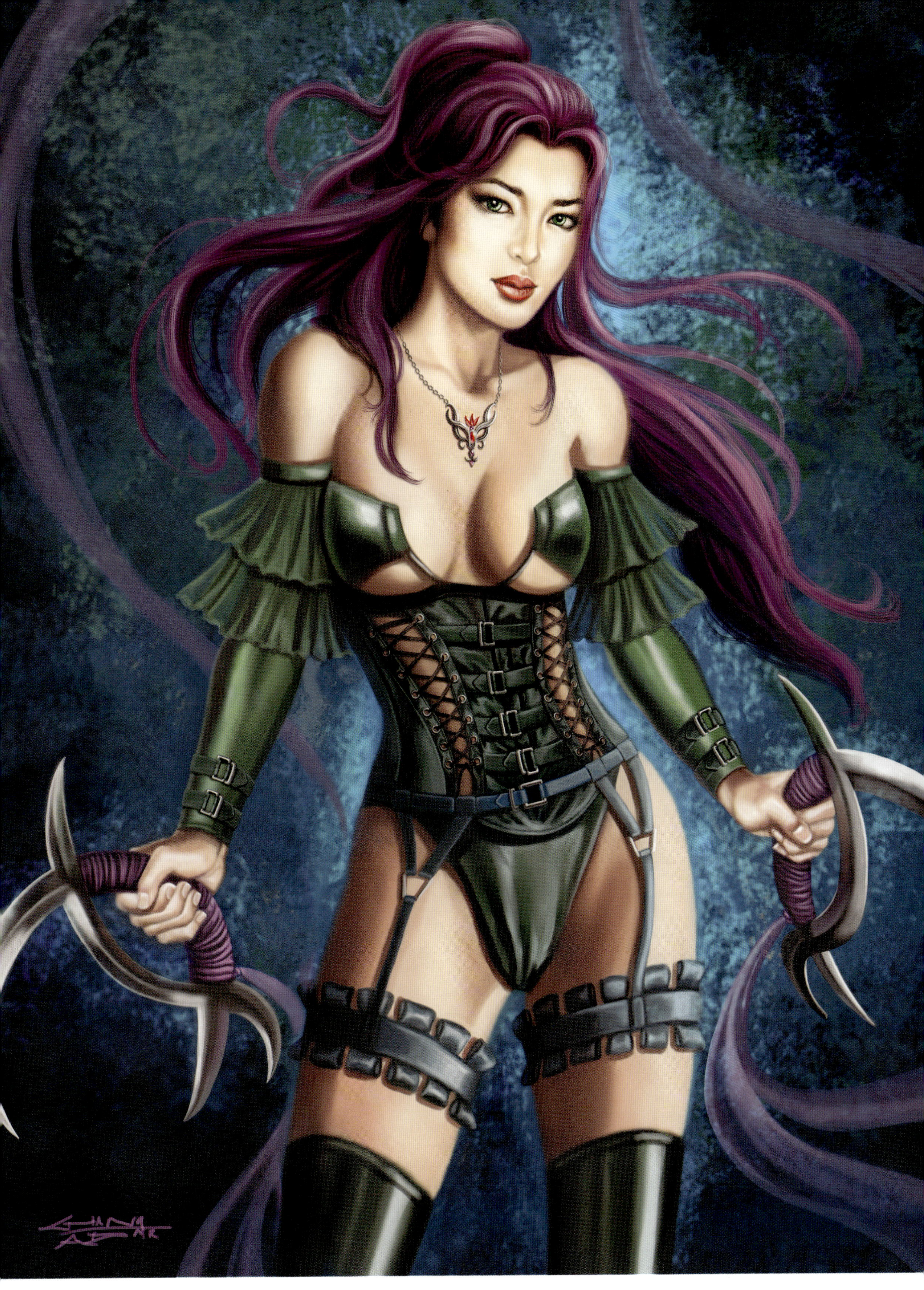

Violent Violet Moon

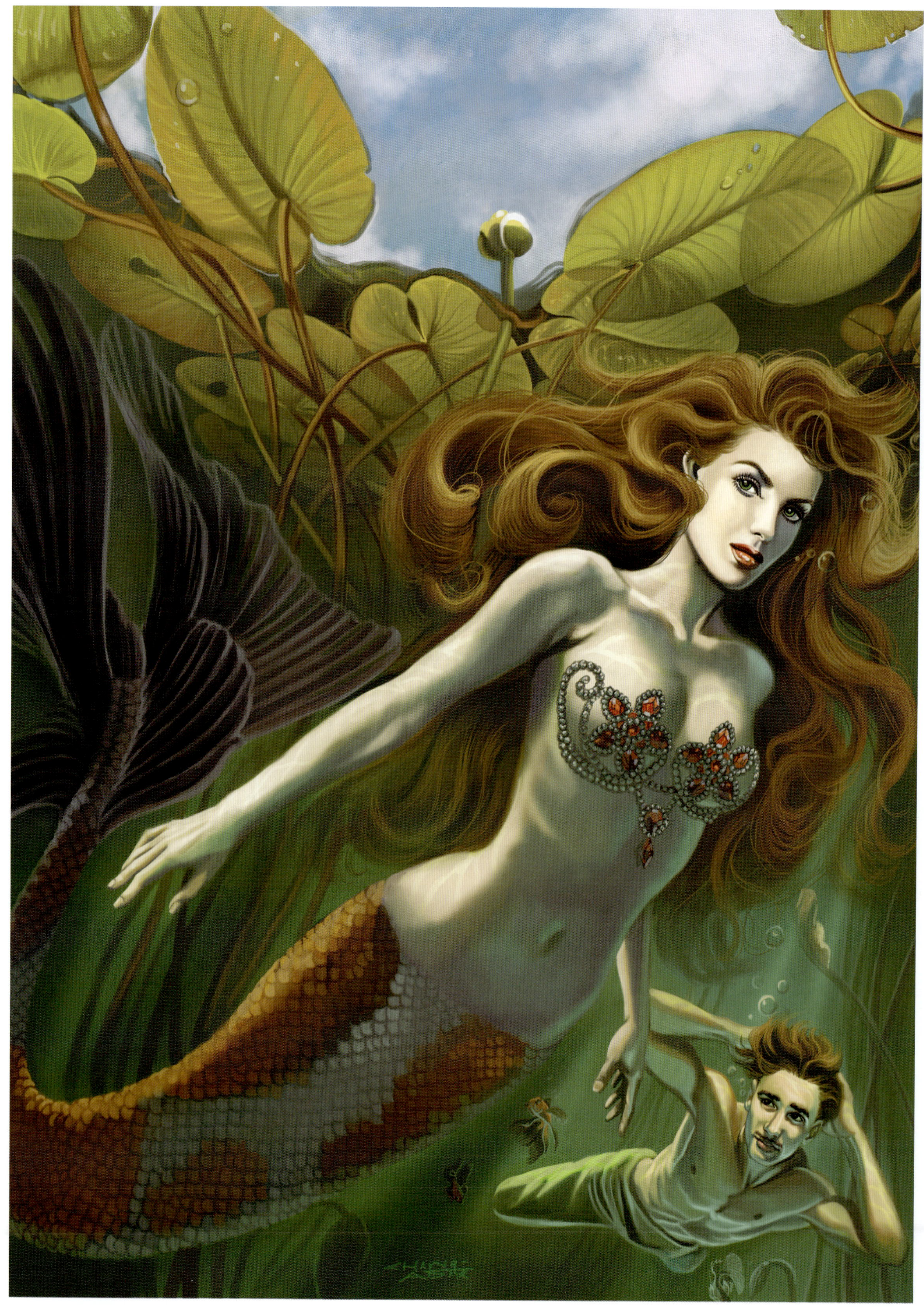

Mischievous Mermaid

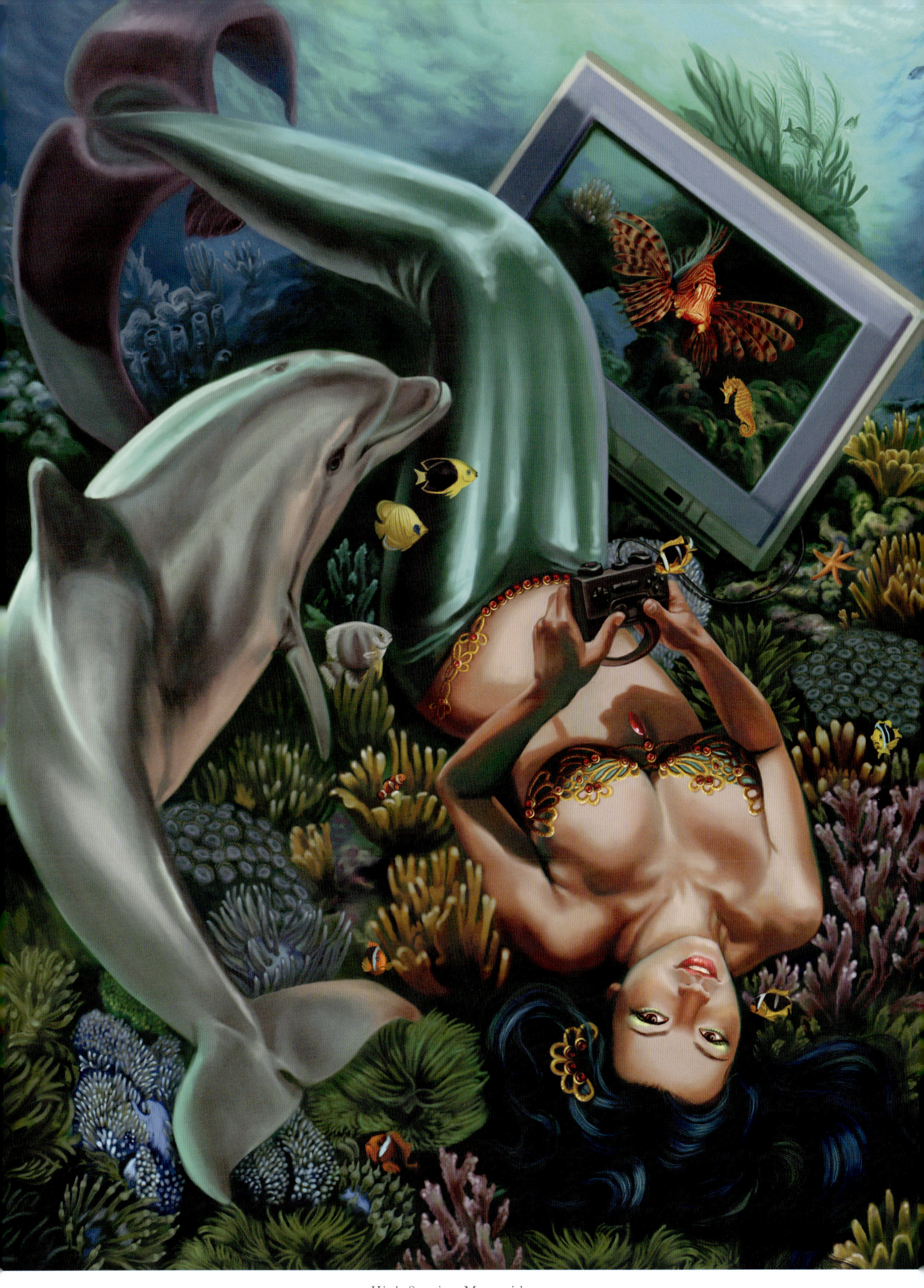

High Scoring Mermaid

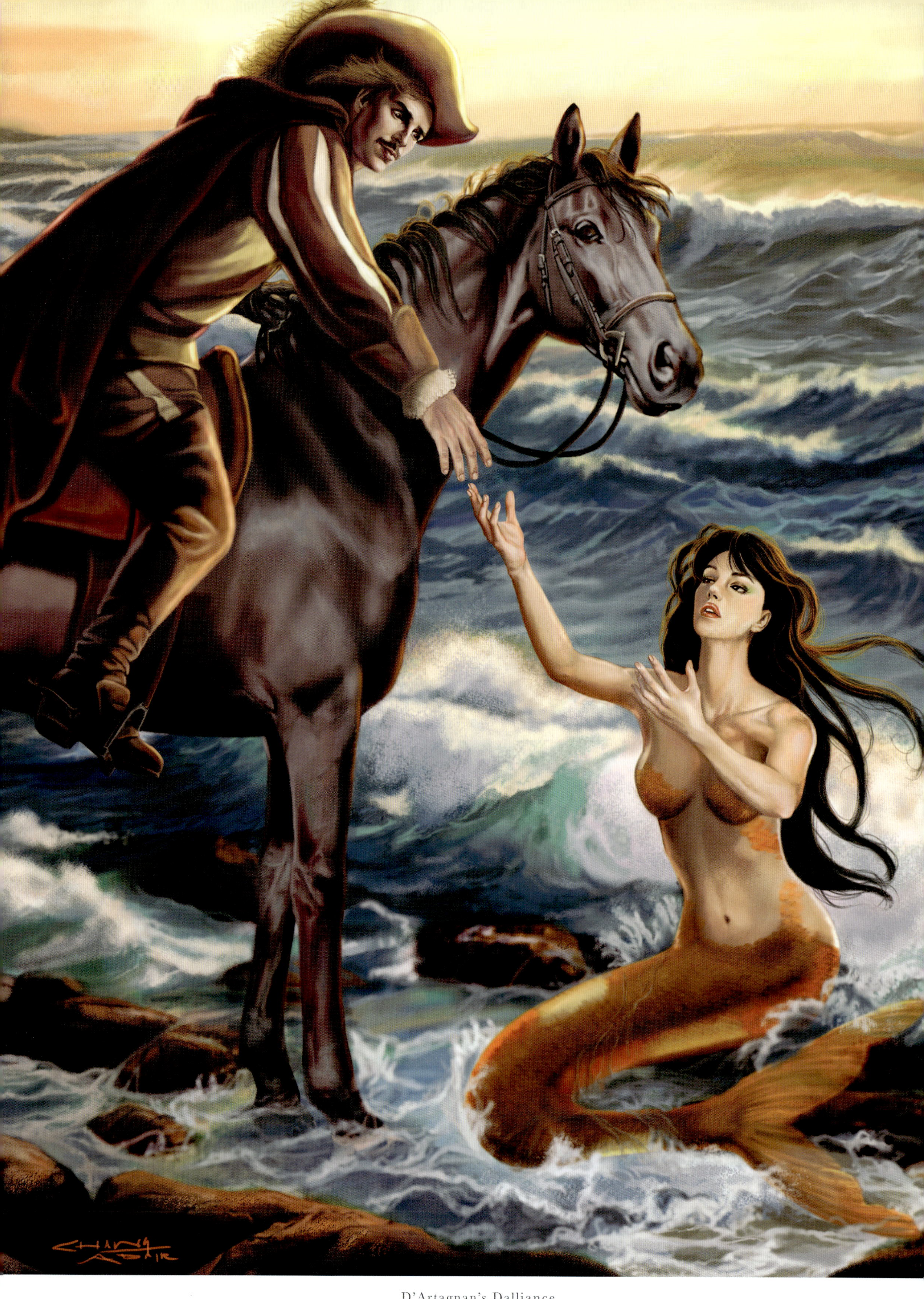

D'Artagnan's Dalliance

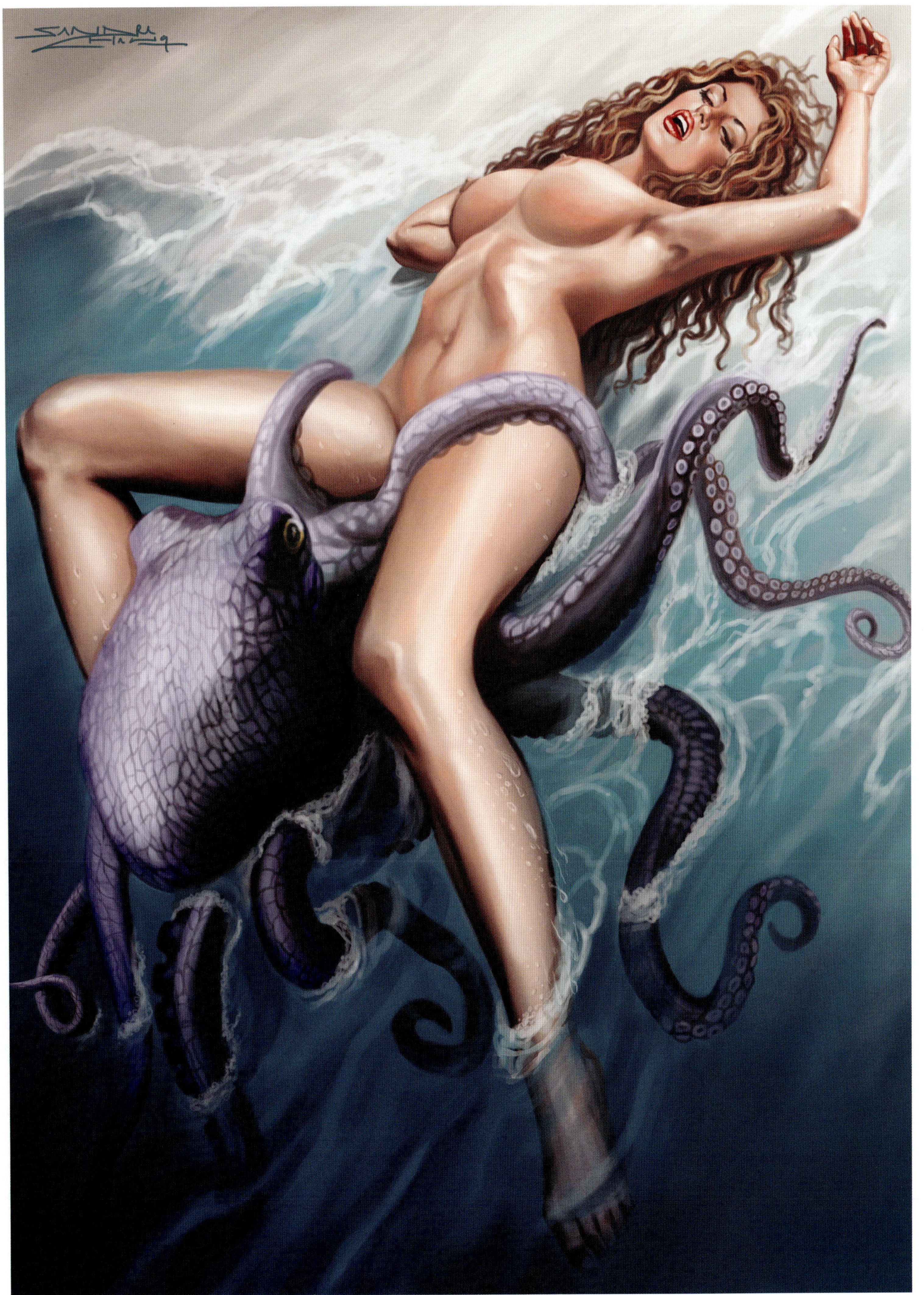

Seduction on the Shore

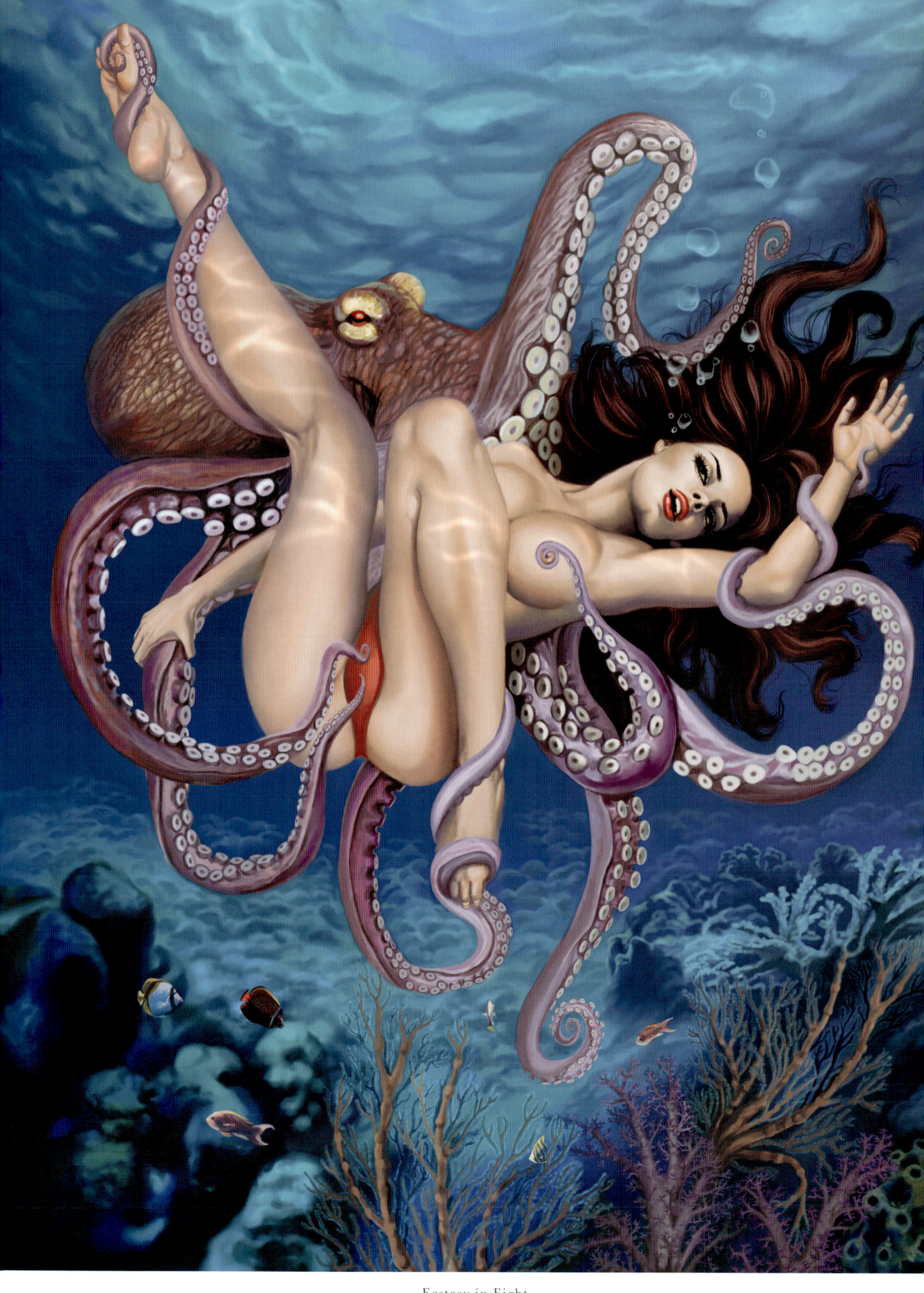

Ecstasy in Eight

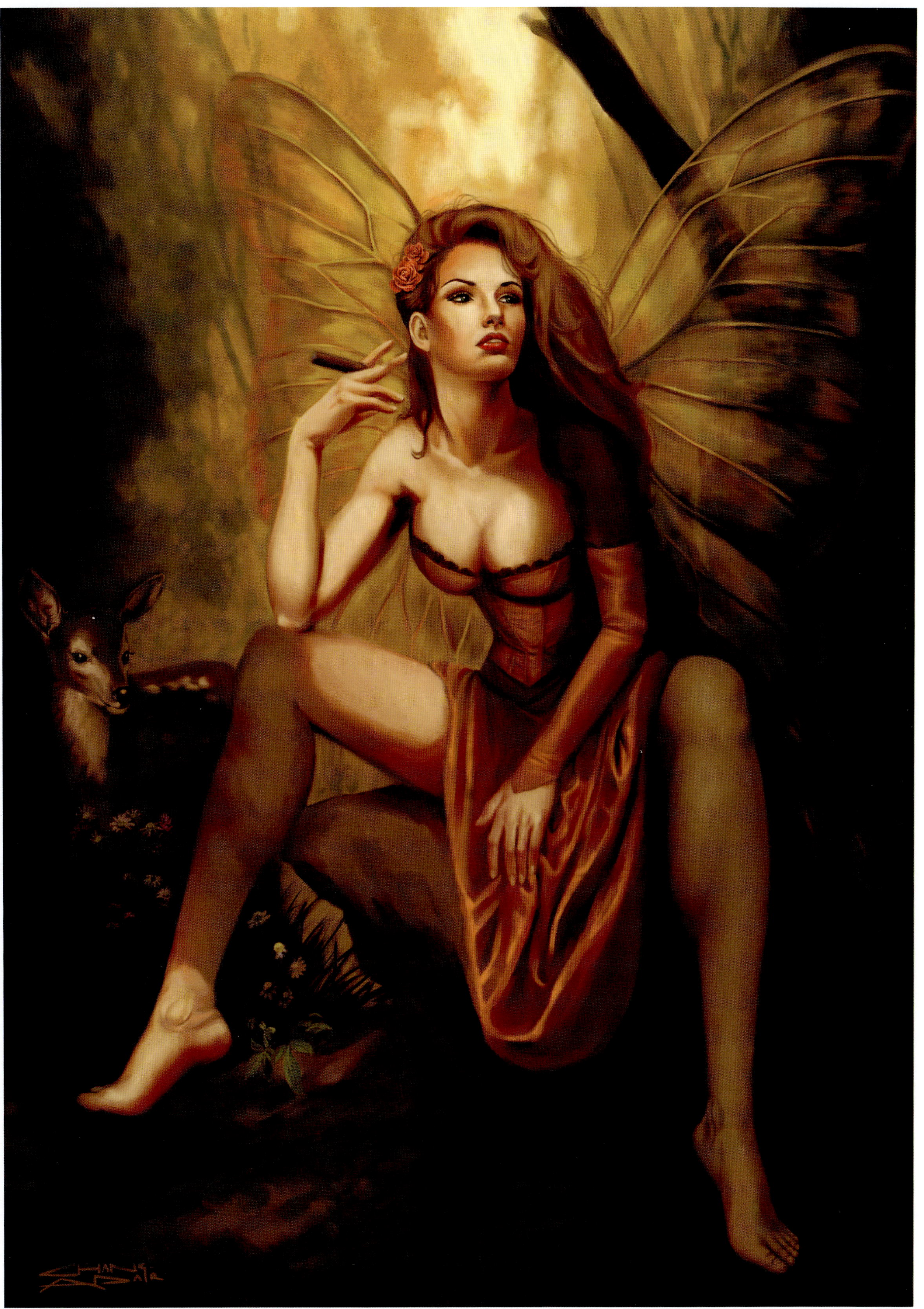

Naughty Faerie

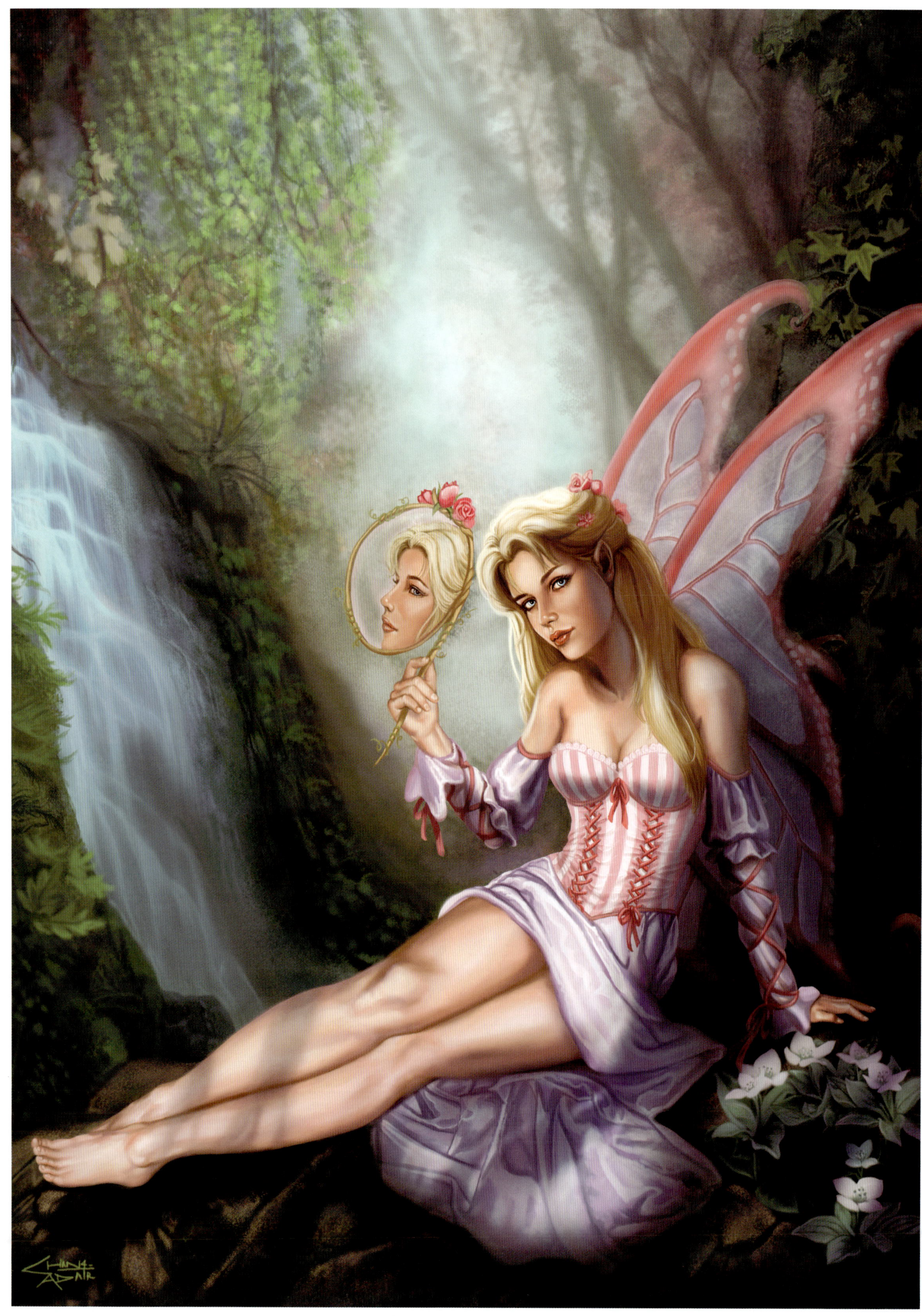

The Faerie's Boudoir

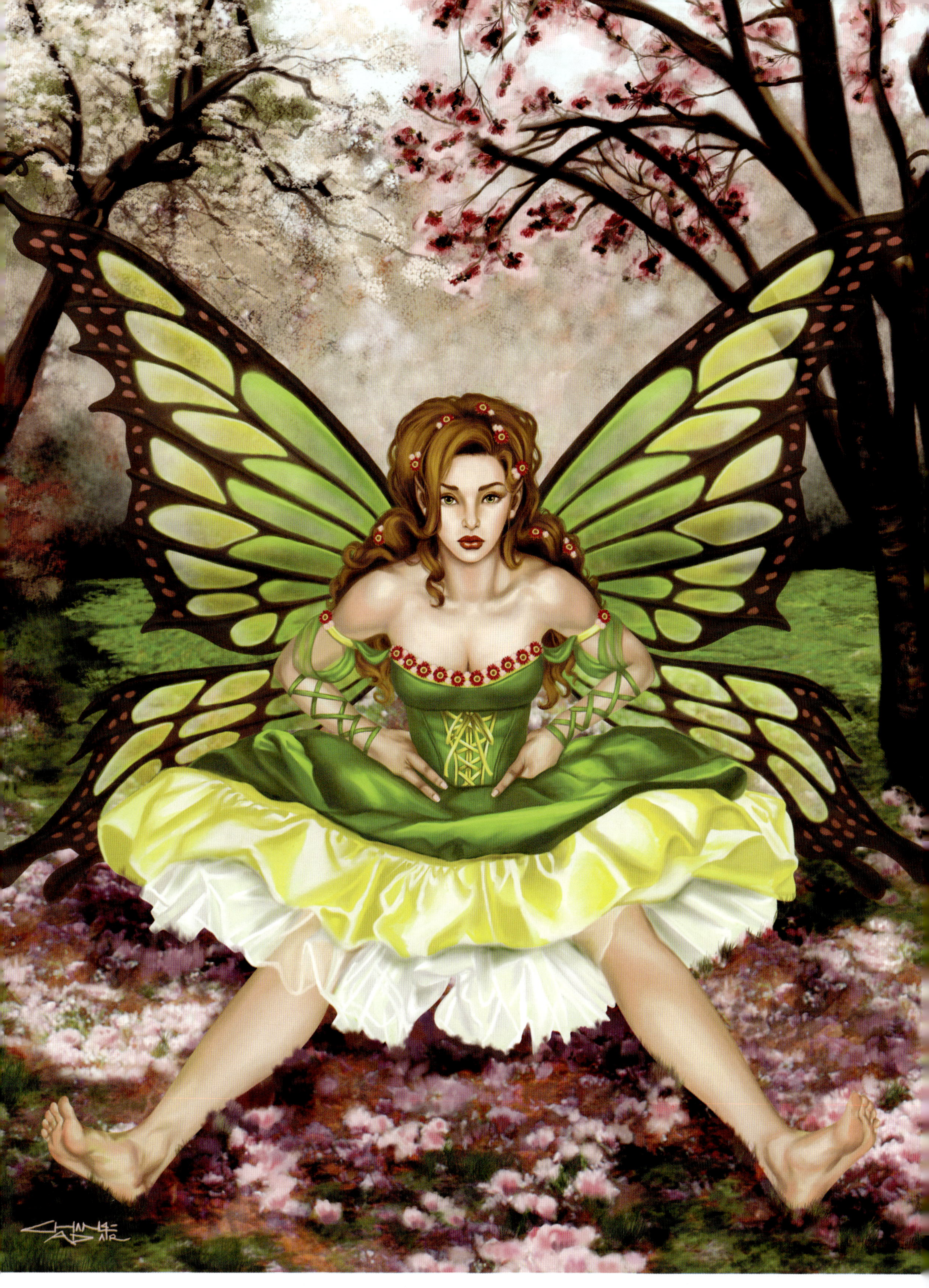

Fiore Faerie

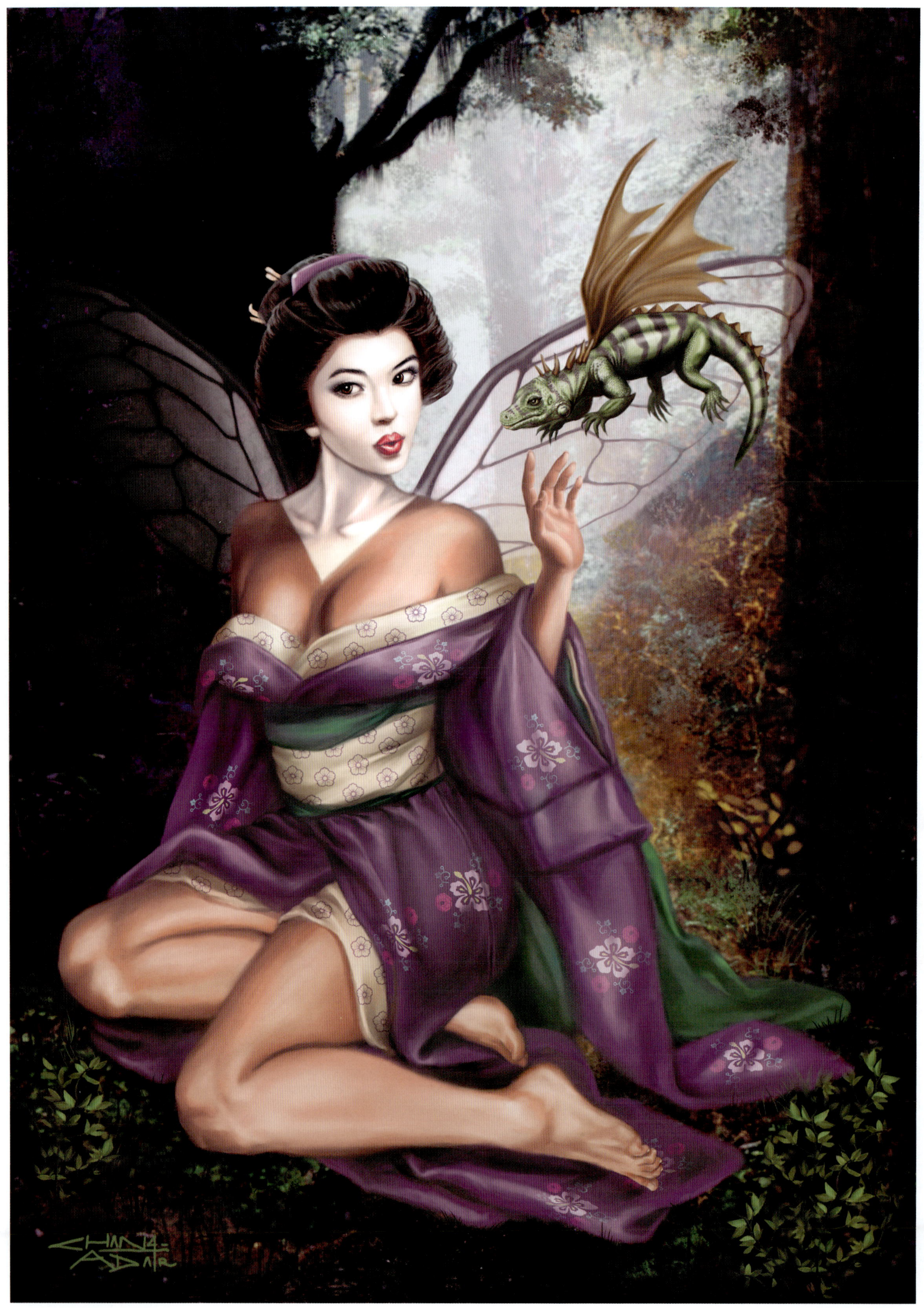

Geisha Faerie

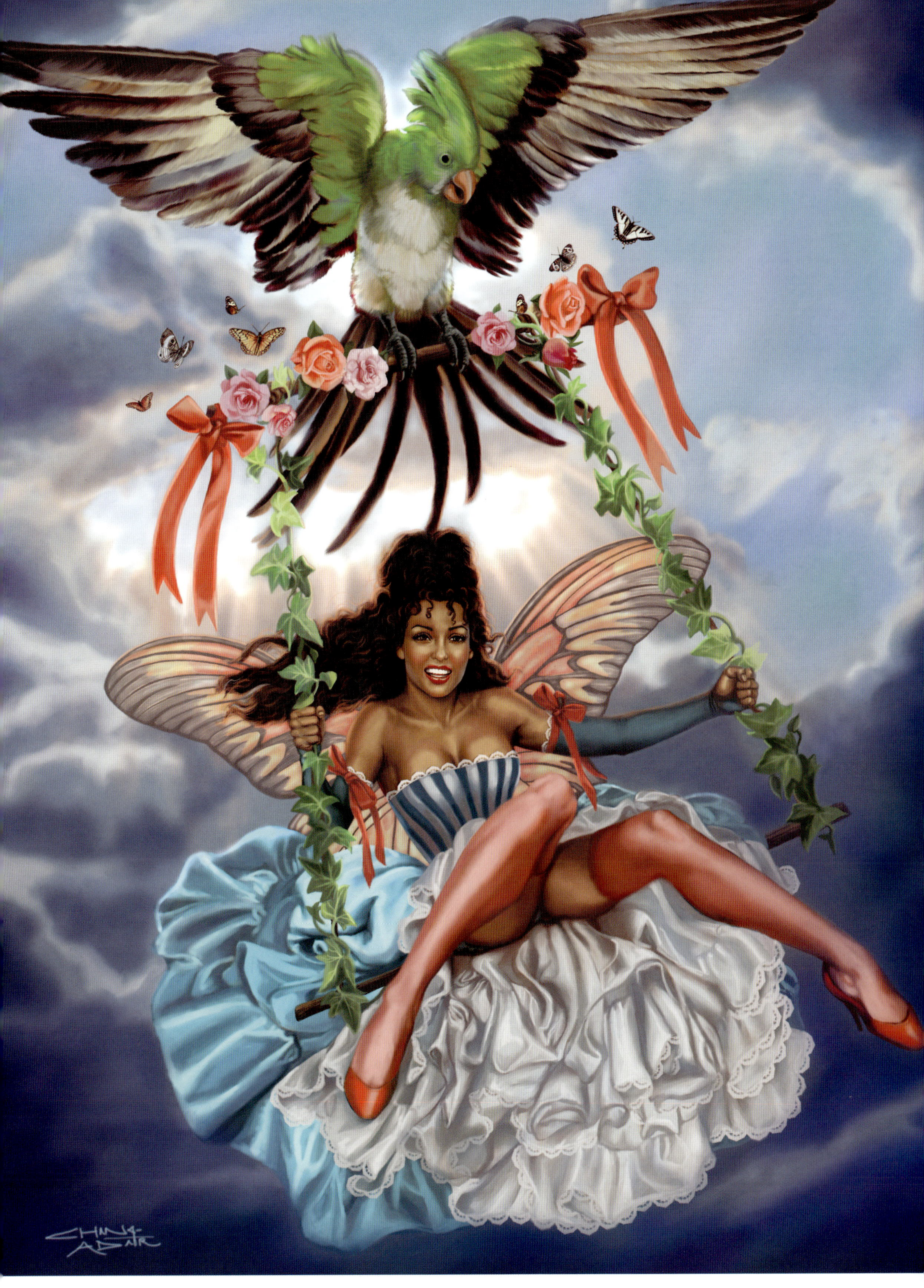

La Dolce Vita

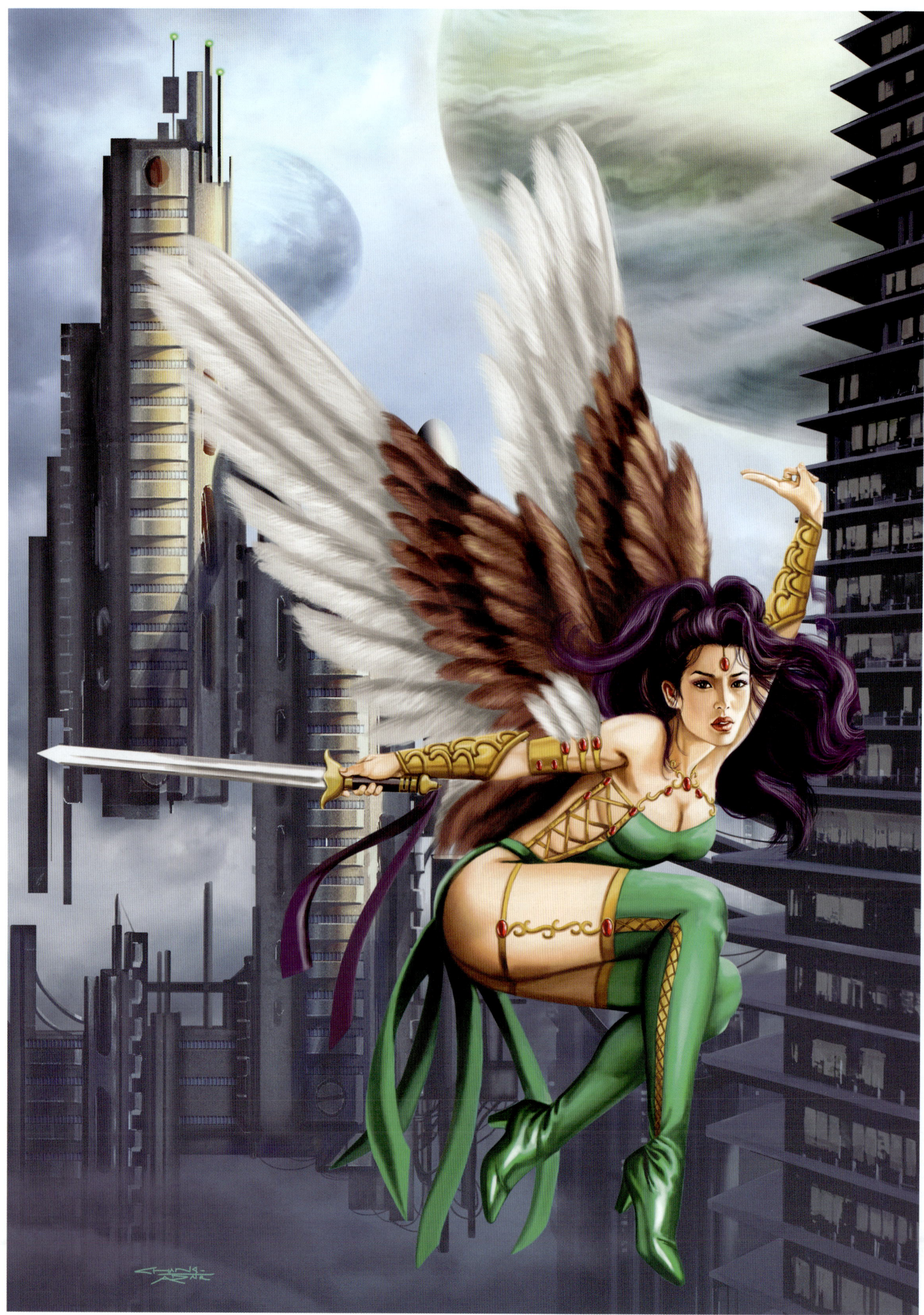

Angel Ambrosia

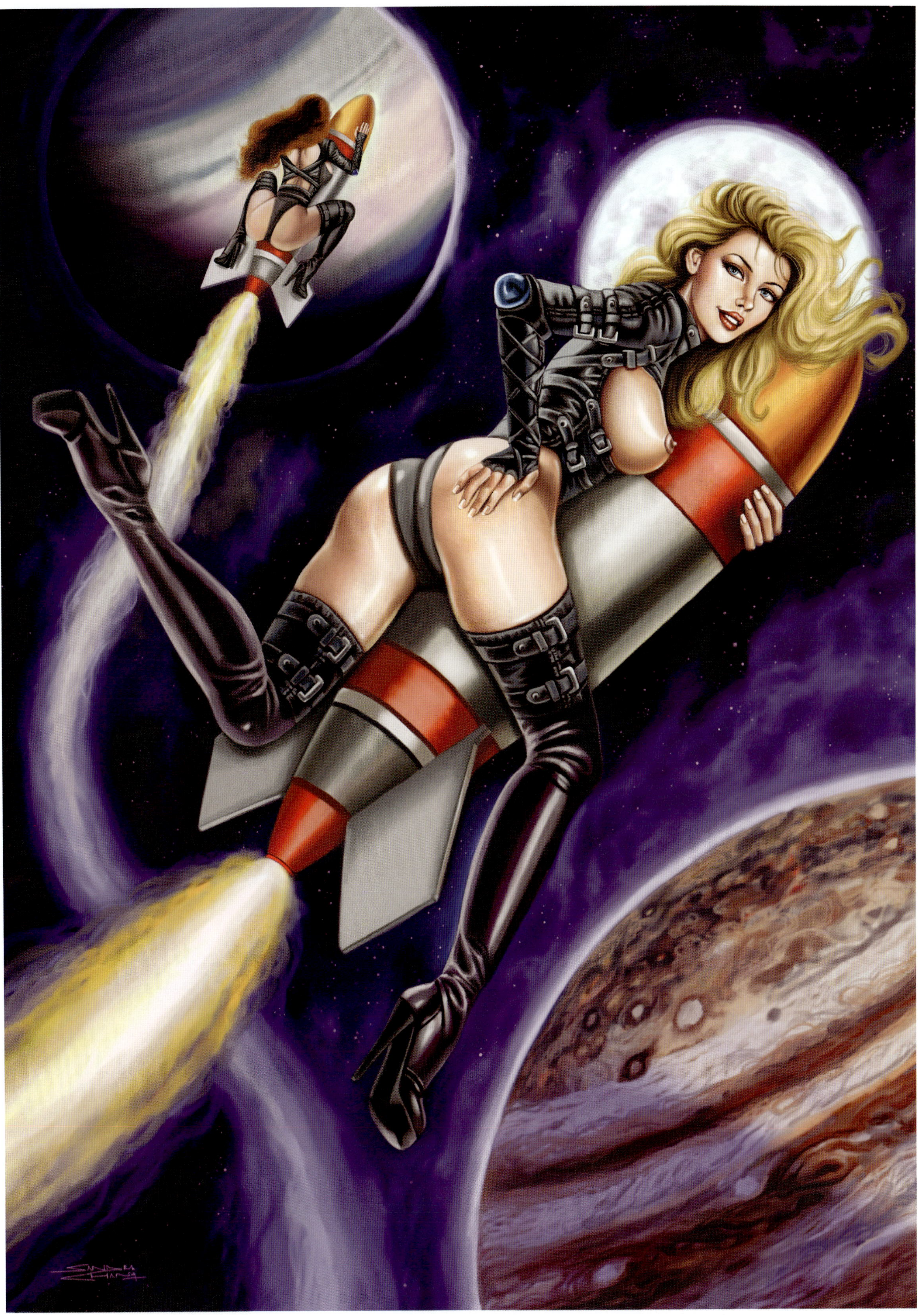

Racy Rocket Girl

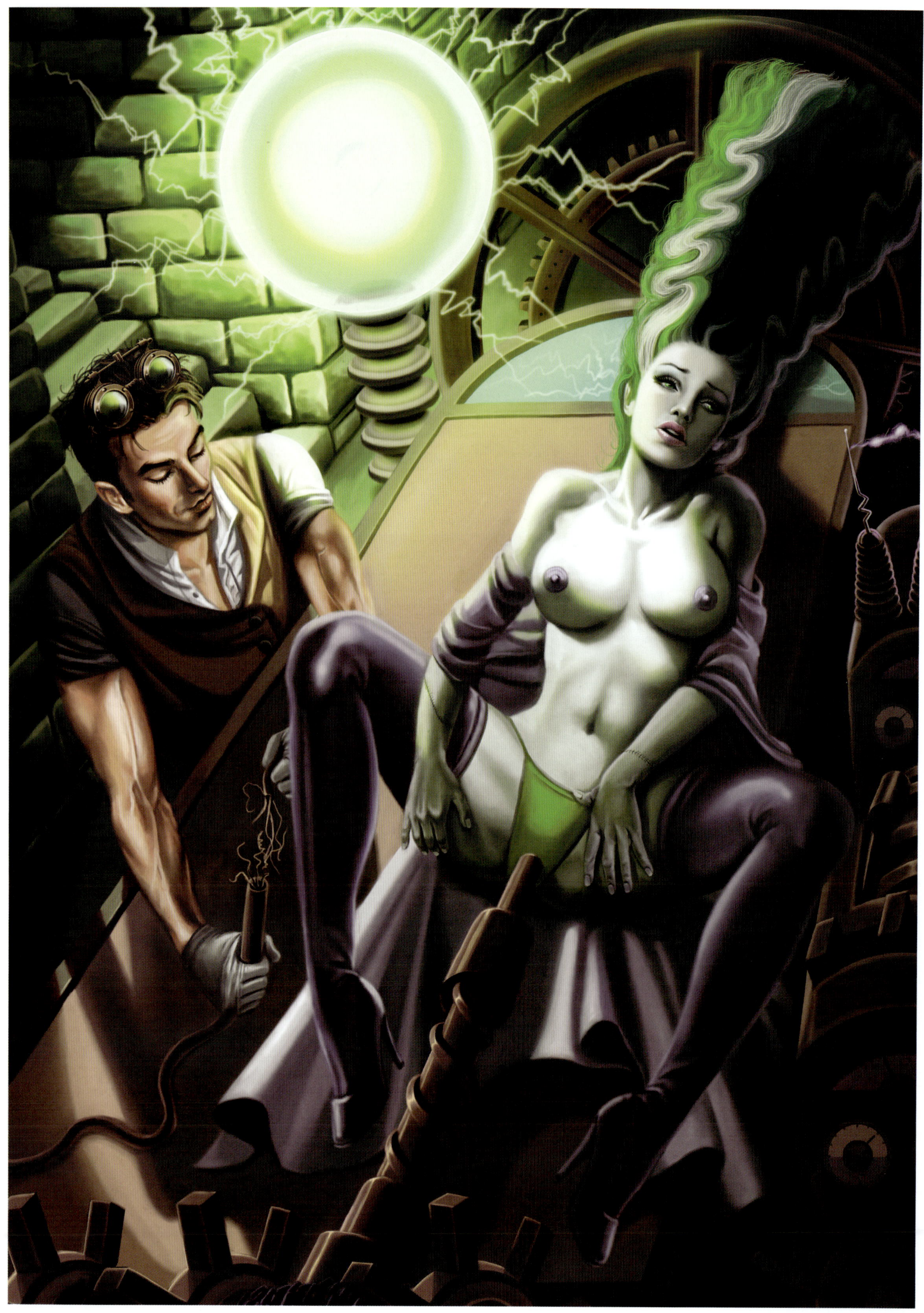

Victor's Lusty Liaison

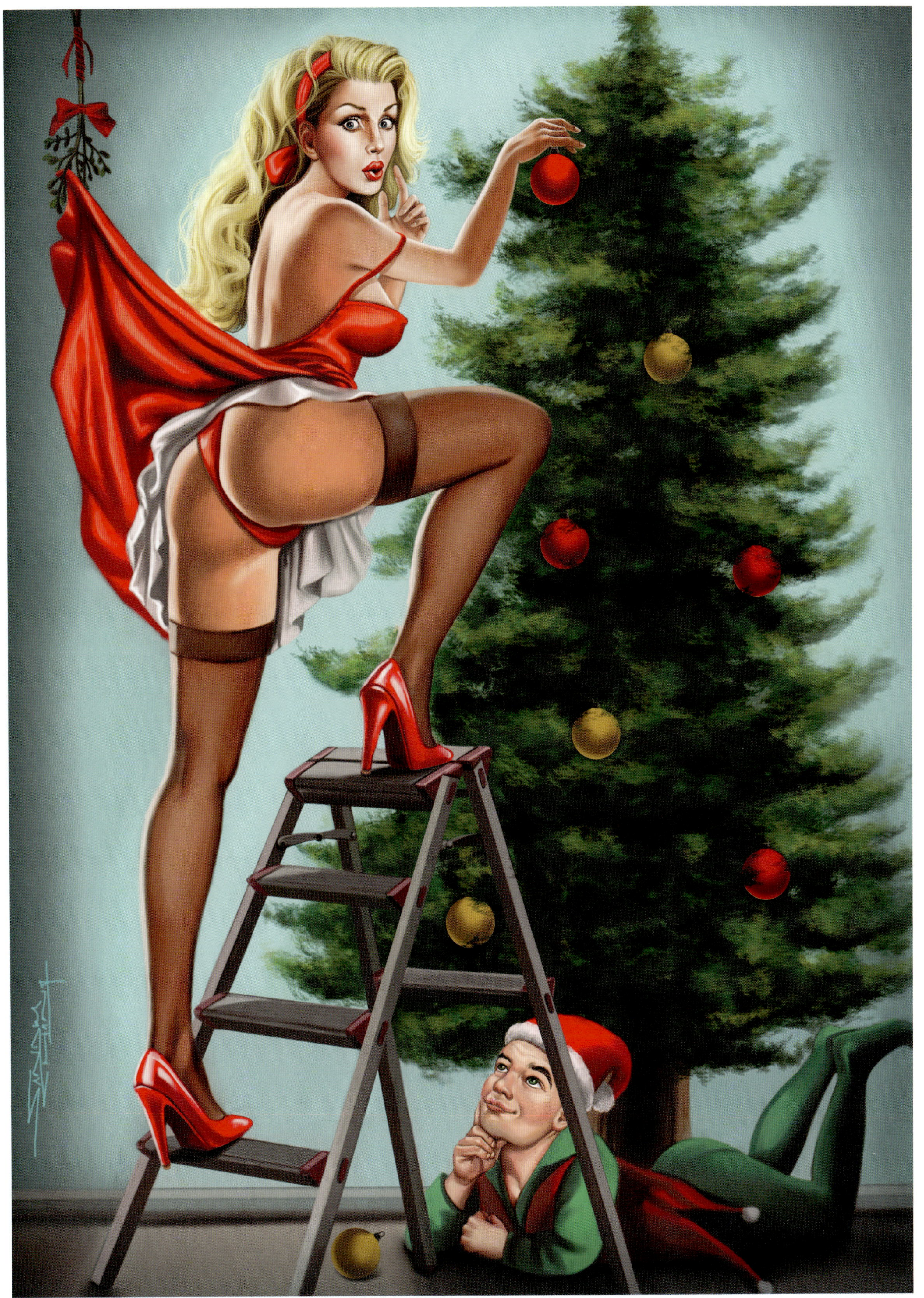

Malicious Mistletoe

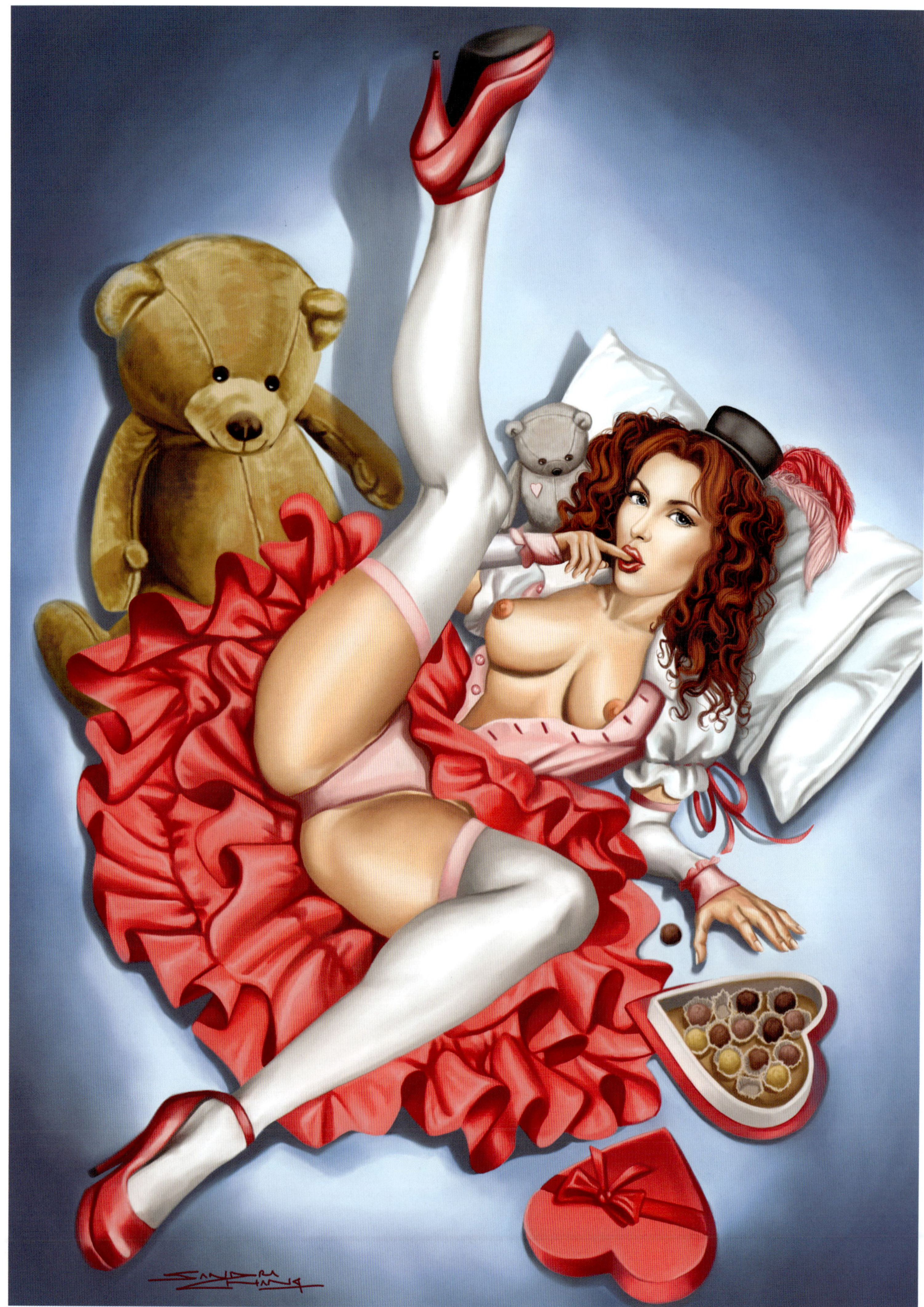

Hot Chocolate

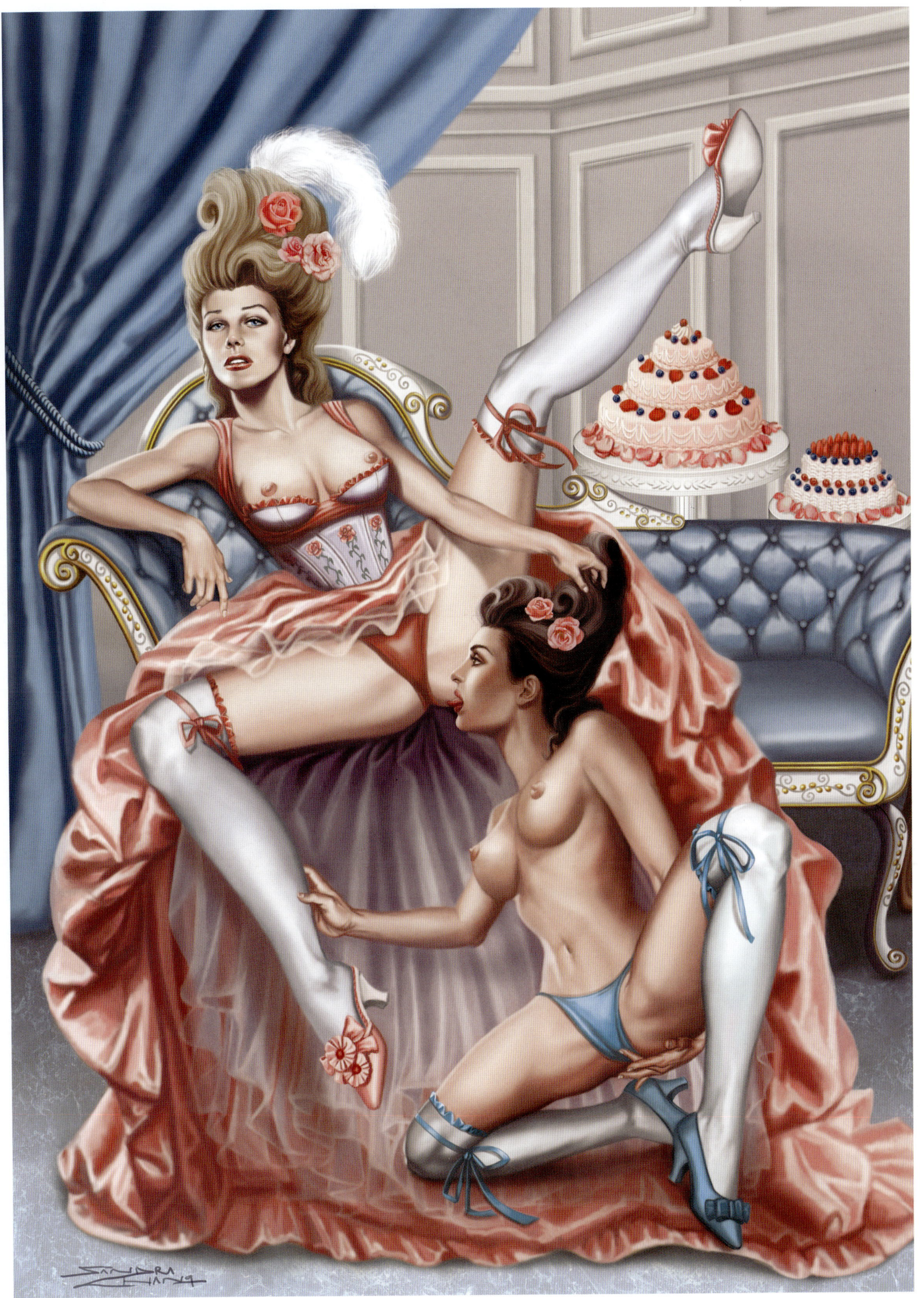

Marie Antoinette's Lady-in-Waiting

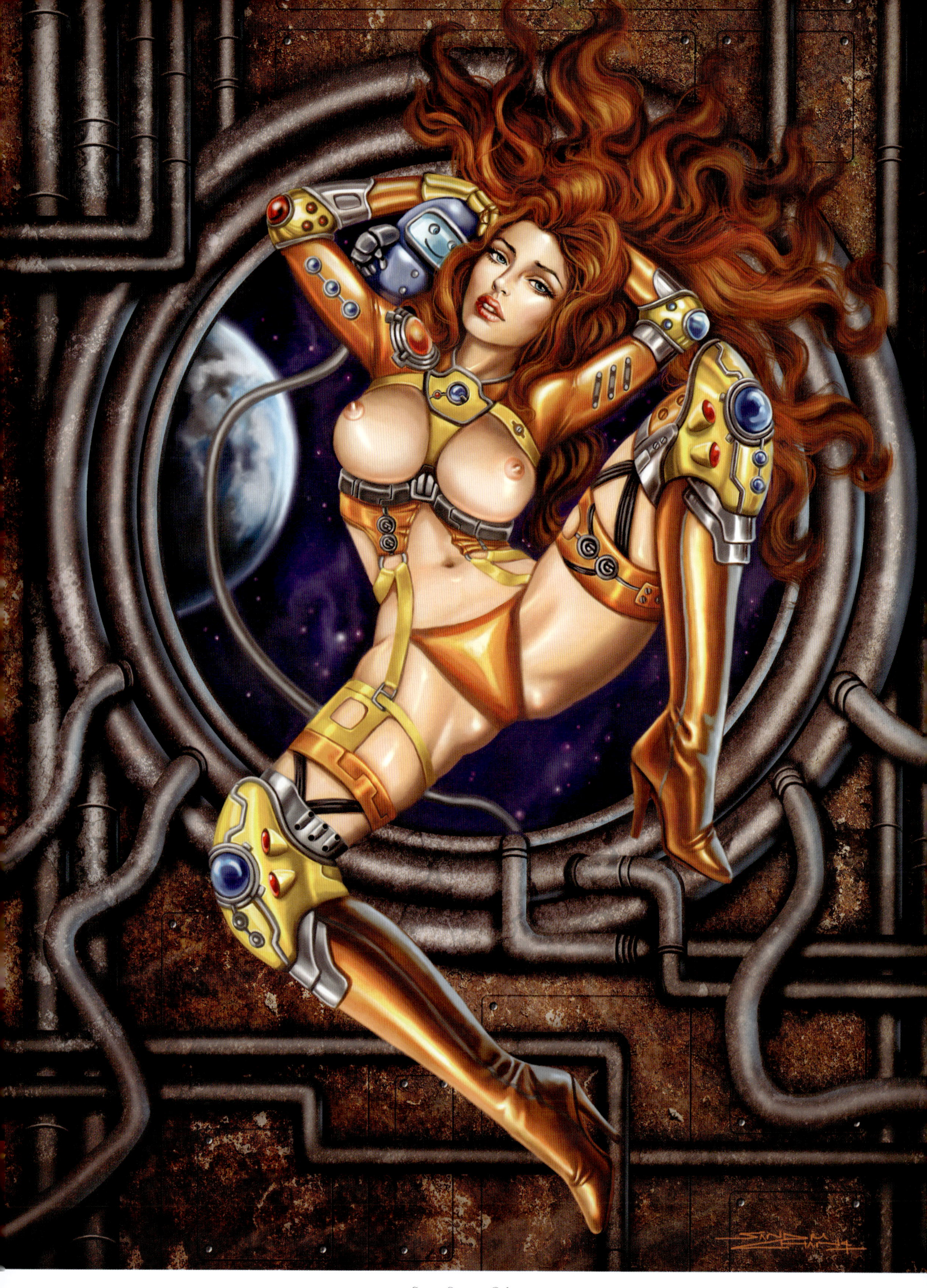

Sexy Space Odyssey

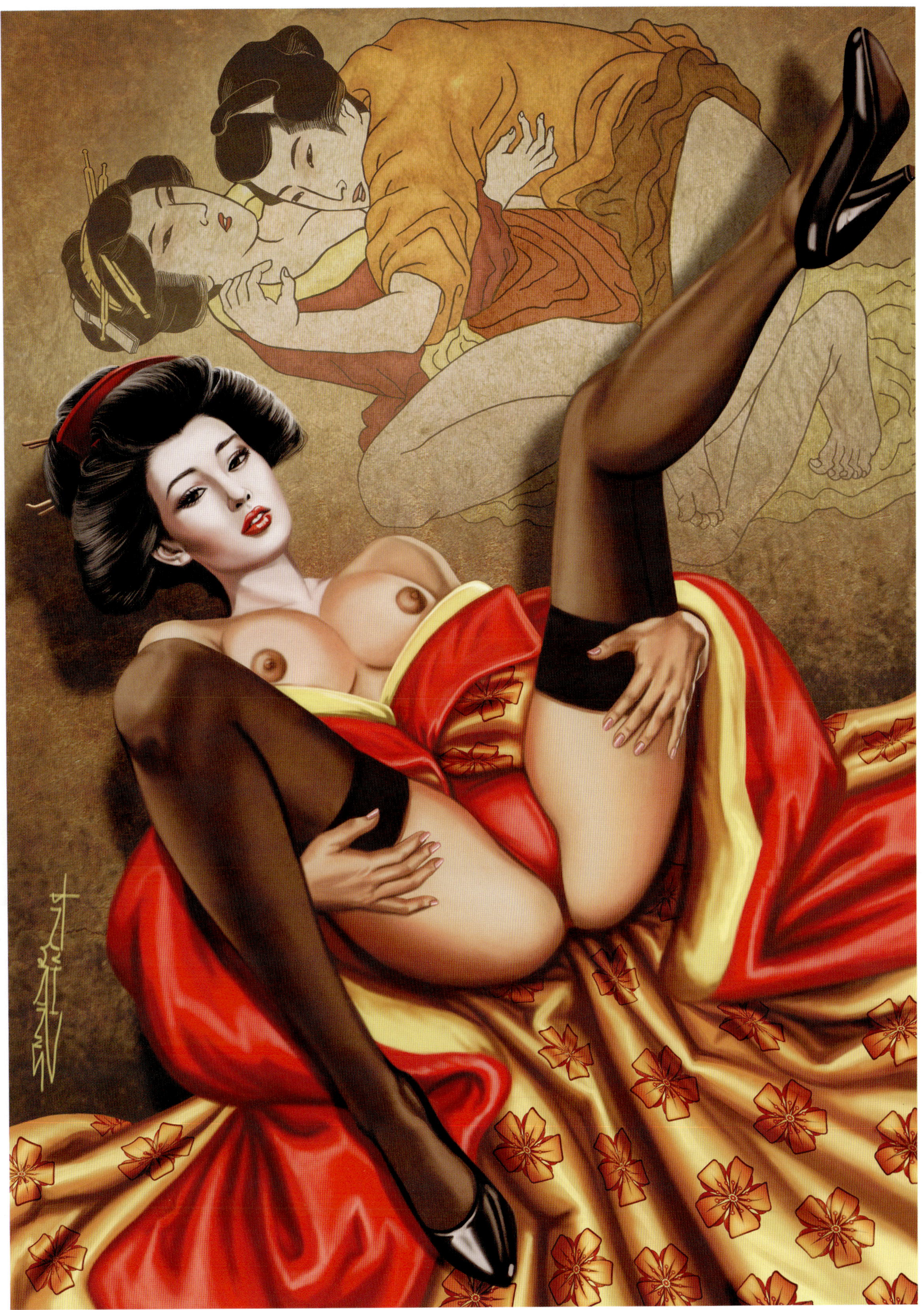

Kinky Kimono

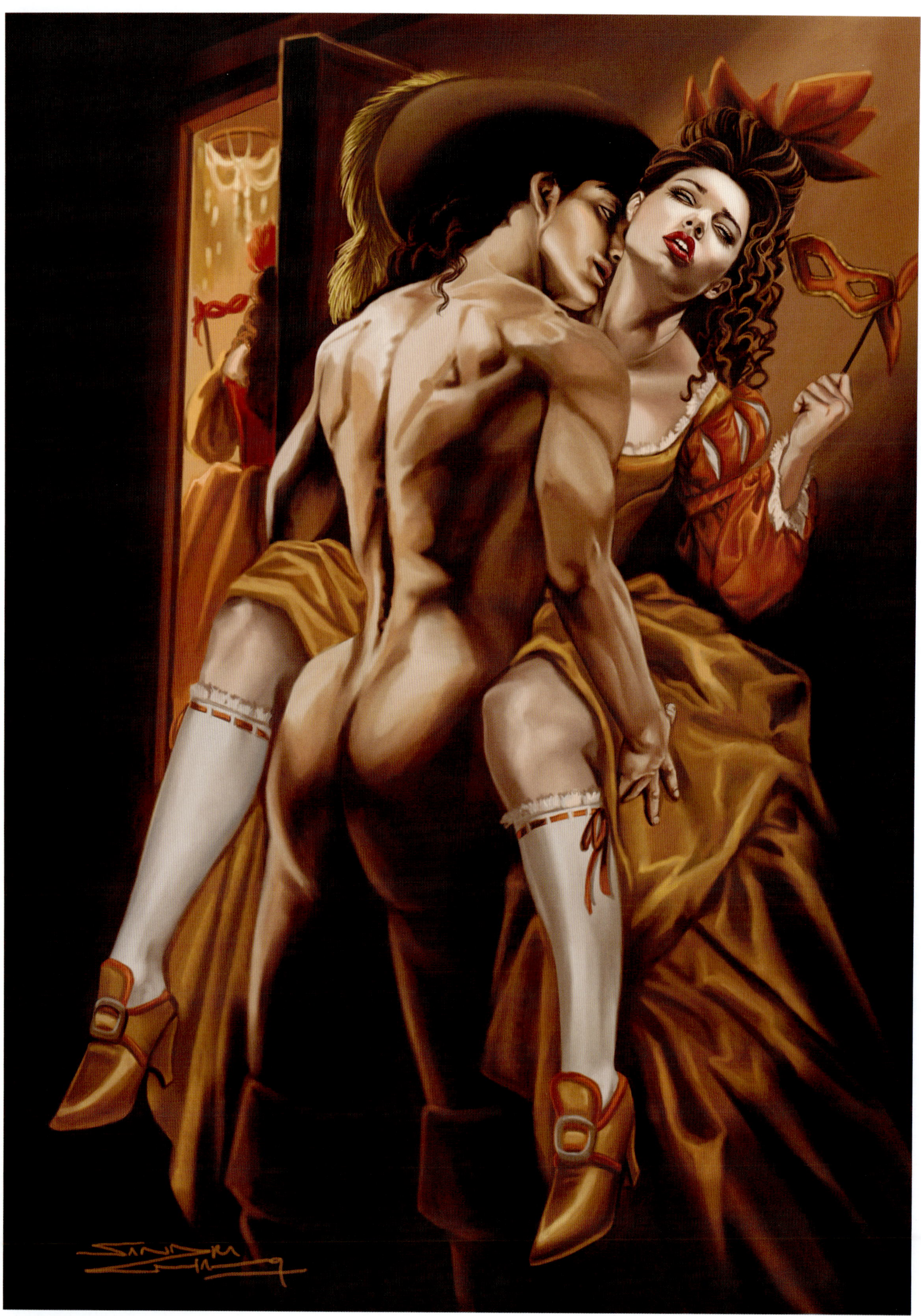

Musketeer Masquerade

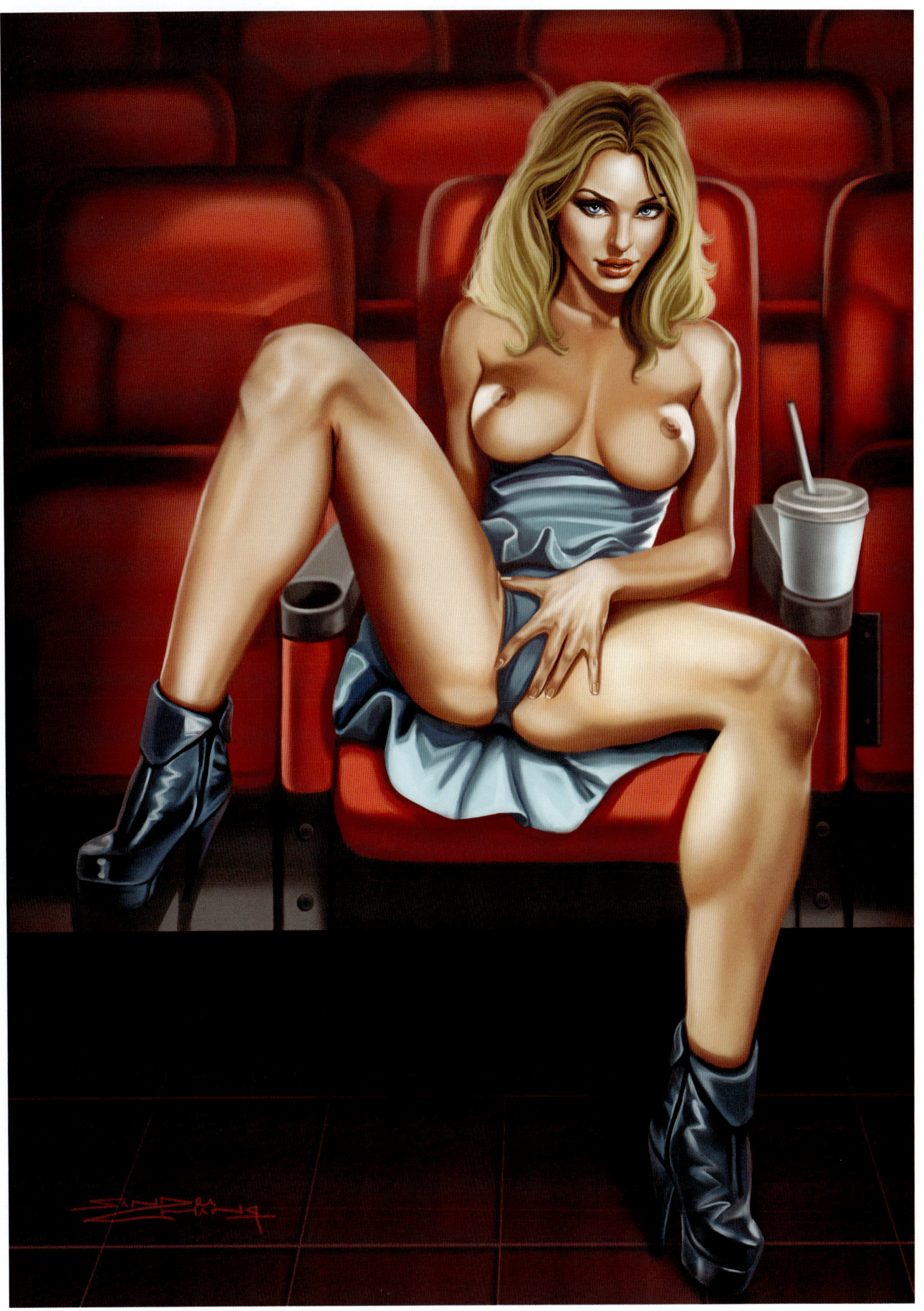

Thank You for Coming, Now Relax and Enjoy the Show

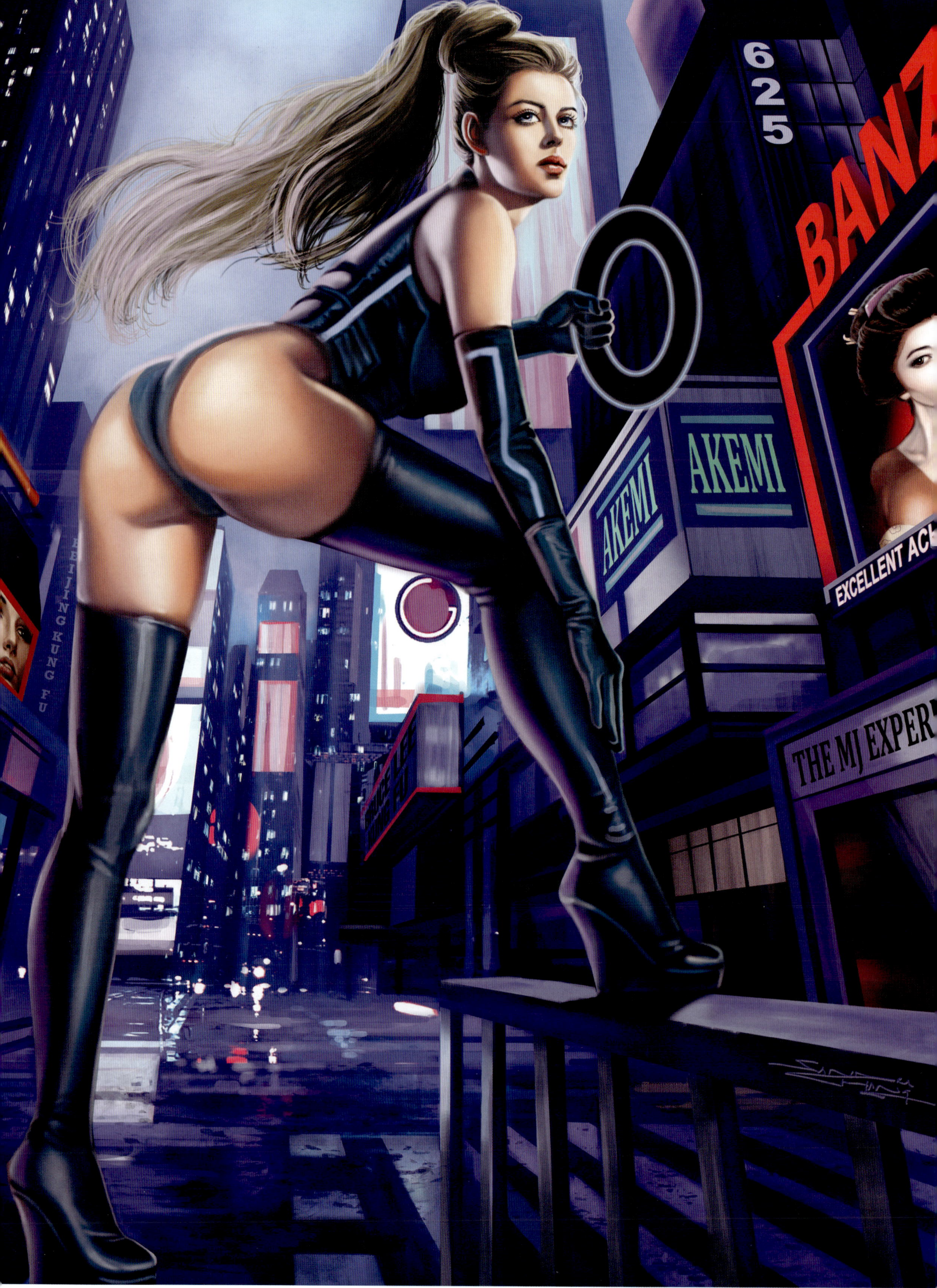

Night Lights